For my old (but still very young) and very dear friend

Uncrowned Queens

Rebecca

Anny Latour

Paris, March 78

Uncrowned Queens

Reines Sans Couronne

By Anny Latour

Translated by A. A. Dent

With twelve illustrations

LONDON: J. M. DENT & SONS LTD

First published in Great Britain 1970

Made in Great Britain
by Cox & Wyman Ltd,
London, Fakenham and Reading
for
J. M. DENT & SONS LTD
Aldine House · Bedford Street · London

SBN 460 07721 X

CONTENTS

CONTENTS

ILLUSTRATIONS

Between pages 84 and *85*

To the memory of my sister

Maria Horch

AUTHOR'S PREFACE

Among the women whom I have sought to bring to life in these pages the reader will find neither queens nor poetesses, nor mistresses of the great. Neither has fame itself crowned them or plaited their laurel wreaths. For all that, they have created kingdoms: and such kingdoms as had their frontiers, their laws, their own peculiar lustre and, under the name of *salon*—nowadays a symbol of outmoded smartness—they once represented a living reality.

In fact for centuries the *salon*, as shaped by certain women conscious of the spirit of their times and immersed in its flood tide, was a state within a state. To ignore it is to lose an indispensable key to the history of civilization. It was the *salon* that shaped the whole concept of urbanity, made criticism effective and opened new paths to art, to literature and often to politics. From this ever-burning hearth were to spring sparks which would set the world ablaze.

The women who presided over *salons* of such moment surely deserve the title of 'uncrowned queens'?

There are women who have won fame by the accident of royal succession, such as Christina of Sweden or Catherine the Great; others by their talents or their beauty, such as Madame de Staël, Madame Récamier, George Sand—who can recall them all? But Madame de Staël promoted her ideal of international liberalism not through her *salon* at Coppet, but by means of her books. George Sand, in answer to a guest at a party who remarked that she was not talking, said: 'You, sir, come here to work; but I come to rest.' Jean Cocteau said of the charming Madame Récamier, who was surrounded and adored by the eminent people of her time, that she so well understood the art of silence that in the end she became the chaise-longue that bears her name. Is that derogatory? There are few people who know how to listen. It is an art in itself, lost today in the babble of the cocktail party.

Thus neither these queens of the pen nor these silent beauties would quite fit the framework of my study. Rather, I shall look among the *salons* for the traces of women who, if less beautiful than these, have had more influence in depth, and whose far-sighted suggestions have shaped the civilization of their time and its evolution.

A way of life is never created by a war or a revolution. Neither kings nor emperors dictate styles. When we say 'Victorian' or 'Louis XIV' or 'Jacobean' we are simply fixing the style in time and space. The truth is that every age receives its stamp from society, a select circle of which promotes new forms in art, in language, in domestic interiors, in fashion. From it and it alone proceeded the slow and mysterious changes whereby Gothic turned into Renaissance, Renaissance into Baroque, and Baroque into Classical. Mechanization has disrupted this progression, so that our era has found its own democratic level in a bare and functional style.

In the Middle Ages, which witnessed the most abundant harvest of the French genius, the troubadours of Provence fashioned with all their poetic invention the henceforward ineradicable image of the *grande dame*. It is her shining image, fleetingly incarnate in certain feminine figures, that we shall pursue throughout this book.

Already in Isabella d'Este the figure of the *grande dame* is expressed as only the cultural absolutism of the Italian Renaissance could create it. The central personality of the great prelude to French classicism is Madame Rambouillet, around whom polite society first took shape and formulated its private language.

The art of conversation is lost in our day, and the *salon* has perished with it. Instead, intellectual research, the pursuit of new techniques for working and living take shape in the course of conferences, consultations and cultural confrontations which attempt to answer all our questions.

Even the idea of the *Grande Dame*, the Great Lady, is a thing of the past. Now that woman goes to work she has become the everyday comrade of man. When Proust created the character of Madame Verdurin he dealt a death blow to the last exemplar of the lady of the *salons*, with her empty ambitions, her affected mannerisms and her snobbish slang.

In my pursuit of these feminine figures who inspired, often in secret, certain great revolutions of the mind I have had to follow their careers, even sometimes their love affairs, step by step. But for the biographer there is a real risk of losing all objectivity, once having penetrated the core of his subject's life and often been fascinated by it. If I have not altogether escaped the perils of such fascination, I crave the reader's pardon.

CHAPTER ONE

THE TROUBADOUR AND THE LADY

THE CULT OF THE VIRGIN MARY AND COURTLY LOVE

The Virgin Mary reigns in the gilded shadows of the chapels. Seated in majesty on a throne, with a cloak of royal blue on the shoulders, crowned and distant, she presents the Infant Jesus to the throng of the faithful. In the Middle Ages it is thus that believers, from Byzantium to the Pyrenees, see her. Thus she appears in painting, in sculpture, drawn in the myriad glittering stones of mosaic. As the Queen of Heaven she is a symbol, exiled in her celestial sphere.

Earth is a vale of tears, humanity is fallible and guilty. No bridge leads from this world here below to the Beyond; from Eve, the image of sin, to Mary, the image of purity. Saint Paul had laid it down: 'Let the women be silent in the assembly.' And certain moralists had gone one better: 'Woman has no soul.'

But from the eleventh century onwards humanity prises itself loose from the bonds of ecclesiastical discipline and sets out in search of its own destiny. The beginning of the twelfth century is marked by a hitherto unknown spiritualized sensuality. Man wants to enjoy life but at the same time attach himself firmly to the Faith; and he turns to art and poetry to show him the way.

This new intellectual and artistic direction, with its subtle moral values, leads to fertile territory. And just as cathedrals, art and poetry emerge from a chaos of war and barbarism to bear witness to a spiritual revival, so at the heart of a feudal class that has become powerful through pillage, abuse of power and acts of piracy a new social concept arises, forming a world apart for the arbiters of moral standards: this is chivalry.

Inaccessible to the outsider, the order of knighthood proclaims purity of morals, faithfulness unto death, courtesy, protection of women and of the weak—chivalrous virtues that will survive until the time, long past our day, when the knight is no more than a figure of legend.

In this refined society woman has reached a high status. Not indeed woman in general, but the *domina*, the great lady, the focus of admiration and the supreme goal. For the man who wishes to win her, more than male virtues are needed: he must have learning, polish, courtesy, skill at the tourney, good table manners and a certain sophistication. Man can rise to this level only when he has learnt to live with dignity.

In the castles and fortified manor houses, far from the towns and the rising burgher class, relations between man and woman have undergone a great change. For the first time women take their place at the banqueting table. The stages of amorous pursuit and coquetry, gentle submission and delicate seduction have created unprecedented refinements: gallantry, the dialogue of love, and elegance of dress.

As Georges Seignobos said, Love is a French invention of the twelfth century. And in fact, this is self-evident. Never before had there been such idealization of women or such ennobling of men by women. The legend of Tristan and Isolde, in which man and woman have the same right to love, the same duty of fidelity, would have been inconceivable in classical antiquity, when love was considered a misfortune, a form of weakness that paralysed the will. The exaltation of love to sublime spheres was undreamed-of. On the other hand, during the Middle Ages love and the cult of devotion to a woman are a source of beatitude.

Now the whole concept of the Virgin changes: she is no longer an inaccessible deity, a heavenly manifestation. Sweet, gracious, tender, motherly, transfigured by her smile, she still lacks some of the features that make up a personality, but already she is an individual, and a feminine one, with a life of her own.

The *domina*, châtelaine of the castle, Madonna reigning in heaven, who shall tell one from the other? The cult of the Virgin and love for woman are amalgamated in the furnace of fervour and humility. The quest for new spiritual values has resulted in the discovery of love. The poems of the troubadours glorifying love are the fanfare of a new era. The *chansons de geste* convey to us the adventure of chivalry, but the songs of the troubadours lay bare for us the singer's inner life, his desires, his love of nature and of God and Woman.

THE TROUBADOUR EXTOLS THE LADY

The minstrels and singers, successors of the actors and mimes of antiquity, had brought into France a highly coloured repertoire of stories, including Celtic legend and the cycle of King Arthur and his Round Table.

However, along with chivalry a new *élite* is born. The ladies of this *élite* will demand more than a pastime, more than the mere recital of heroic adventures: the minstrel must be not only a performer, he must also be a creative poet, an inventor. Thus 'troubadour', from *trovare*, comes to mean 'he who finds'.

The Romantic Revival seized on the figure of the troubadour; the same literary school which produced the figure of the poet starving in a garret *à la* Chatterton also popularized the concept of the poor medieval poet, or minstrel, singing his love songs under the window of some lady who has been shut up by a jealous husband.

Historical reality has a quite different look. The troubadour had high social status and a good education—often, indeed, he ranked as a scholar, as often again was of noble birth. But in the cases where he was of baser extraction, he had but one ambition—to be admitted to feudal society; and this was more important to him than what we should nowadays call critical acclaim. A poem dedicated to the lady of a castle might be the means of gaining him a post on the establishment of that castle. In the southern provinces of France the first flowers of this new-style poetry will be plucked. Up to now the poet has been a nameless, faceless figure, but now he has an identity, can be a celebrity just like his contemporaries in painting and sculpture and architecture.

Now who were these noble ladies of whom, to whom, the troubadours sang? Few of their names are known to us. Eleanor of Aquitaine, wife of Henry II and mother of Richard I of England, was the most famous, and scholars and poets thronged most thickly about her. For fifteen years she was Queen of France until her husband Louis VII repudiated her for loving not wisely but too widely. It is above all to her that we owe the spread of Provençal courtliness into the northern, Franco-Norman sphere. Marcabru, Bernard de Ventadour and Jaufré Rudel, the poet of the *Princesse lointaine*, wrote for her.

But the so-called 'Courts of Love', where real sentences were pronounced, are only a creation of fantasy. It is vain to look for any sign of their existence in the writings of the time. It was André le Chapelain who invented this poetic fiction: in a work composed about the year 1200 he described the 'Court of Love' and drew up for it a code of thirty-one articles. His work is interesting as a typical specimen, showing all the symbolism of the time, and the whole philosophy of love with its manifold subtleties, its sophisticated interpretations, a very mirror of feudal high society and its tone: significant, too, of its decadence.

The last quarter of the twelfth century saw the unfolding of an international civilization of gallantry and courtly poetry. But while in the German language area the Minnelied flourished, society in France was undergoing profound changes. The rites of chivalry, deprived of their original meaning, degenerated into fashionable ceremony. Feudalism was decaying, its influence waning as the power of the monarchy waxed. Chivalry had played out its social part to the end, and now was fit to sustain nothing more than a new style in art and literature.

THE LADY DETHRONED

The world of artistic creation can expand only on the basis of a stable society. If its roots lack soil, it will become dislodged and alienated from tangible reality. This happened about the middle of the thirteenth century, and again in our day.

In the first part of the *Roman de la Rose*—the part which Guillaume de Lorris wrote about 1240—poetry still shines as in a many-coloured mosaic. It was to serve as the model for a literary convention that went to, and beyond, the limits of the absurd. But the day of courtly lyricism is already past, and so is the cult of Woman; literature is about to become the expression of a new society.

Forty years—forty significant years—later, Jean de Meung will add another eighteen thousand lines to the original four thousand.

But what a change of tone! Jean de Meung is a misogynist. He has put down the Lady from her throne, overturned the pedestal on which his forerunners placed her. What is the reason for this revolution?

We are coming into a new stage of history. The houses that formerly clustered round the castle for protection are now regrouping into villages and towns. A middle class is establishing itself with the aid of privileges granted by the king. As early as the second half of the thirteenth century, trades for women are taking shape, such as weaving, embroidery, dressmaking, tailoring. The wife devotes herself to household duties which defy glorification, and which only the philistines of the nineteenth century can promote into virtues. The new middle class, very down-to-earth, finds in woman just what the Church had always found: vanity, coquetry, cupidity, infidelity and a mania for display.

Christine de Pisan waged a desperate war, that was doomed to failure in advance, against this literature of misogyny. She was born in Venice in 1364, but brought up from a child at the French Court. Sustained by a mystical ideal which the highly spiritualized Italian poems imparted, she lived in perpetual conflict with her environment.

Her last poem, the 'Dittié sur Jeanne d'Arc', restores her hope of a genuine rehabilitation of woman. She exclaims: 'Hé, quel honneur au féminin sexe!'—but in vain. She cannot put back woman to her old status of *domina*, and all the heroism of Joan of Arc cannot overcome the prevailing misogyny.

But the glory of the *grande dame* crosses every frontier, and with the troubadours of Provence infiltrates through Italy down to Sicily where Frederick II holds Court. The poetic genius of Italy comes to life right in the midst of the political distractions, the feuds of great lords, the pillaging of the *condottieri*. The poets of courtly love, bringing with them the treasures of another civilization, find a welcome and awaken an echo there. At the courts of the petty princes, literary centres are created, and especially at Ferrara, seat of the Este dynasty, the ladies of which, urbane and accomplished, surround themselves with poets and scholars.

The mantle of the vagrant *trovatori* falls on the settled poets. A new language, the *dolce stil nuovo*, is created, a completely new medium capable of rendering courtly love with much more subtlety. Dante, who may have studied at Paris, and Petrarch, brought up in Provence, are both successors to the chivalrous ideal of the troubadours. Dante, who is guided towards the highest spirituality by the eternal feminine, places Beatrice, his earthly love, in the highest sphere of his Paradise.

But with the Renaissance in Italy comes something new. The noble lady descends from her pinnacle and, as a woman, celebrates a joyous resurrection. The poetry of love leaves the courts of the rural nobility and enters the enlightened society of the towns, it becomes the *canzone* celebrating the beloved. Even the image of the Madonna, the inaccessible *Regina Coeli*, undergoes a transformation into a very earthy, very secular Virgin Mary modelled on a citizen's wife or on some woman of the people, an affectionate and tender mother.

CHAPTER TWO

ISABELLA D'ESTE—'THE FIRST LADY OF THE WORLD'

PRELUDE: THE COURTIER AND THE GENTLEWOMAN

It is a spring evening in 1507. Guidobaldo, Duke of Montefeltro, and his wife Elisabetta have bidden to their castle of Urbino a select circle of guests: humanists, scholars, poets, playwrights, men and women of wit. There are few among them without some heavy burden of guilt: most have done away with some enemy by poison or the hired sword. But here in this chosen spot all baseness is banished: nothing counts but nobility of soul, elevation of spirit.

Among the Duke's guests is Count Baldassare Castiglione. Whether or not he takes part in the conversation, not a word escapes him. What is said here will form the framework of his *Book of the Courtier*, not to be published until 1528, but thereafter to serve as the oracle of sophisticated manners to a European society in search of a new way of life.

In it Castiglione as Master of the Revels puts on the stage the men of the Court of Urbino: Pietro Bembo, the great humanist, Giuliano de' Medici, Francesco Maria della Rovere, the heir to Montefeltro and the future son-in-law of Isabella d'Este, Bibbiena, author of comedies and later a cardinal; and many others.

That was a marvellous time, when people in quest of absolute beauty were transfigured in the reflection of that ideal. It is true that no one had been able to get away from the antique standards of perfection, but the Renaissance, by investing the notion of perfection with its aesthetic splendours, made it seem new again. Of these fervent aspirations, what remains today?

Castiglione's dialogues offer a complete picture of Renaissance man: he is no longer subject to transcendental forces, no longer the passive object of divine providence. He acts according to his own free will, guided by his reason alone. Classical antiquity in its time had known this liberty too, with all the scope that it gave genius to develop. But it was only man that was free. By extending this moral freedom to woman also the Italian Renaissance released a rare burgeoning of energy and mental potential.

Civilizations at their height have created in all countries certain idealized types of man and woman. In the seventeenth century France gave birth to the *honnête homme*, and his feminine counterpart. The Italian Renaissance presents us with the image of the *cortegiano* and the *gentildonna*. To Castiglione belongs the honour of having given literary form to their aesthetic mission and the catalogue of their virtues.

The courtier, as Castiglione shows him, is a man of the sixteenth century, of the fully mature Renaissance. *Cortegiano* and *gentildonna* mark the highest point of an age where formal beauty reigned, in the perfection of social poise and sophistication.

In the *Book of the Courtier* we see the *gentildonna* and all that goes to make her. Her supreme task is one of display. She owes it to herself to be intelligent and well informed, to be aware of art and literature and to be mistress of a discreet and charming urbanity, and above all to know how to entertain men by witty conversation. But it is her essential quality to create a harmony, like music, between speech and beauty and graciousness: *musica è donna amata.*

Education, so necessary for an accomplished woman, is received in a convent. There she learns Latin, even Greek, and gets some acquaintance with the classical authors; it is not uncommon to find women who can read Homer and Virgil in the original. Their critical sense grows sharper with learning, until they learn to distinguish between mediocrity and genuine worth. They preside over debate and controversy, exchange ideas with cultivated men, in short they are capable of sustaining a brilliant conversation which is the essence of high society, a supreme art which a hundred years later will cross the frontier into France.

But also, women are expected to have a virile spirit. The term *virago* is a compliment, a flattering term for women like Isabella d'Este, for it signifies a combination of will and heroic virtue, in the sense in which antiquity prized it.

Not only at the courts of princes but also in middle-class

circles women were surrounded by scholars and philosophers. As in antiquity, the courtesans threw up their intellectual *élite*: Tullia d'Aragona, Imperia, a remarkably learned Roman, Veronica Franco at Venice—all these were sung by the poets and noted for the quality of their wit. They owned considerable libraries and art collections, and lived in villas and palaces. In more than one case the atmosphere of their establishments was one of decency and charm, and that at a time when the private life of cardinals and prelates was the raw material for scandalous memoirs.

Moreover, aristocratic society by no means condemned the cynical or the lascivious. The higher clergy, even the popes, found them matter for mirth. Often poems and obscene epigrams issued from the same pen, and the works of Aretino, now confined to the locked shelves of libraries, then circulated freely among the literate public. The great ladies of the Renaissance took pleasure in questionable anecdotes: for example, Isabella d'Este herself, whose letters abound in coarse words and licentious observations, even though at the same time she is maintaining that books and pictures should be dedicated to the glorification of chastity.

It is indeed a contradictory age. Who would have dared to demand that a woman's private life should be irreproachable? But on the other hand she could not afford to neglect her share of religious observances, on pain of being denounced. Courage and learning and social acceptability made up one unit of life, which was not to be confused with religious observance.

The debates about woman which are so characteristic of the period concern her moral and physical qualities and her social obligations. There are several treatises on the subject, apparently of no great scope, but still forming an integral part of the moral standards of the Italian Renaissance. They deal in more than practical advice; they establish a canon of feminine beauty, they attempt to correct nature, and thereby they become the very expression of that perpetual quest for harmony and perfection.

This new myth finds its complete synthesis in Isabella d'Este. Beautiful, gracious, witty, cultivated, of sovereign will and utterly feminine diplomacy, the *gentildonna par excellence*, she personifies the complex but totally harmonious life of her period.

ISABELLA D'ESTE, MARCHIONESS OF MANTUA

The castle of Mantua is devoid of life. Like a lagoon, the muddy waters of the Mincio spread out before the front of the building, which overlooks the park. What silence, what loneliness reign in the halls and galleries, how bare are the walls that once were hung with Titians and Mantegnas and Correggios! In its countless corridors and rooms, only the woodwork, the chimney-pieces and the painted ceilings bear witness to the life of bygone times. But here in the bridal chamber, the *camera degli sposi*, we find a miracle of portraiture. Before our eyes the lords and princes of the Gonzaga family, with their wives, their children and their friends, parade life-size, as they were in the most momentous days of their lives. These frescoes by Mantegna, like a mirage, seem so tangibly close to us that we can almost believe that it was only yesterday the Marquess Federigo and Margaret of Brandenburg kept their wedding feast here.

And who is this child with such strangely Negroid features? It is Francesco, elder son of Federigo, and heir to the marquisate of Mantua. He was to be the husband of Isabella d'Este, *prima donna del mondo*.

The crowd, raving with enthusiasm, parts before the stately procession: the young couple on their white horses, followed by their train, ride under the triumphal arches which themselves are masterpieces of impromptu architecture, to which the best painters have put their hand. Isabella is sixteen, and Francesco is eight years her senior; they are to be married at Ferrara Cathedral on the twelfth of February 1490.

The solemn entry into Mantua takes place three days later. Here too the town is decorated with triumphal arches, flags, carpets hung from windows, and here too the people are wild with delight. Thirteen mules follow the procession, heavily loaded with splendidly painted chests and presses containing Isabella's elaborate trousseau, with her robes of state and jewellery.

What can she have looked like, how can we reconstruct her beauty, which so many poets sang? The drawing done by Leonardo da Vinci several years later shows us her aristocratic profile, at once delicate and forceful, her hair falling in soft waves on her shoulders. The Marquess of Mantua, ill-endowed by nature, is really very ugly, with his bulging eyes, bulging forehead, splayed nose, blubber lips. His is the world of horse and hound, he lives for war and hunting.

Was ever a more ill-assorted couple than this Francesco and Isabella d'Este? They have been promised to each other for years past. Their marriage was arranged when Isabella was only six, for the contract was ratified on the fourteenth of May 1480. The young boy was sent to Ferrara immediately afterwards, so that, in the words of a diplomatic dispatch, 'they should fall in love with each other'.

The Este archives have preserved Isabella's letters, in stiff and childish writing, to her betrothed. When she was only ten she asked Francesco to send her the famous Mantuan dancing master 'that I may see him dance and hear him make music'.

All her life Isabella's character will be stamped with the absolutism of the Este princes. All her political actions will be soaked in it. From them she inherited a proud awareness of her rank, and from them that royal perspective which ignores everything except what serves to enhance her prestige.

For the house of Este, power must be expressed in terms of splendour and magnificence. Even today their residence, the Castello Vecchio, and their summer palace of Schifanoia, with their splendid frescoes, reflect their liking for the grand and majestic.

Fortunately the princes of Este had ambitions that went beyond war and revelry; they sent out the call for intellectuals, and filled their court with physicians, jurists, astrologers, poets and artists. But Ferrarese society did not by a long way resemble the idyll described by nineteenth-century historians. This was a stormy age, and the civilized life of monarchs was lived at the expense of their subjects, their humanism flourished at the cost of humanity. Except for a few of the most celebrated, scholars, poets and artists lived under lamentable conditions. Documents from the Ferrarese archives have recently brought to light many petitions in which artists who have decorated churches and palaces to the glory of the princes beg for financial help to succour their families in pressing need. But who is concerned with their poverty?

Before her marriage Isabella was able to witness the revival of the classical theatre. It is all to the credit of Prince Ercole that in

1487 he put on the *Menaechmi* of Plautus and the *Amphitryon* of Terence. In the castle of Ferrara he improvised a stage with scenery of painted wood, representing houses, trees, rocks, one of the first Renaissance stage settings, in a style that was to remain valid for centuries. It was to serve as a model for Isabella's theatre at Mantua.

The cultural dowry which the young Marchioness brought to Mantua fell on fertile ground. Marquess Ludovico, patron of the arts, had been served by Leone Battista Alberti and Donatello; and for decades Mantegna worked for the Gonzagas, while the famous Vittorino da Feltre had made Mantua a centre of humanist learning.

In the vast castle with its countless staircases, corridors, halls and hanging gardens, Isabella chose the ground floor for her private apartments. There she took refuge from the noisy life of the Court and there she was from the beginning sure of a quiet retreat in her *studiolo*.

Right from the first year of her marriage she kept up a huge correspondence, as no woman had done before her. Her letters are spontaneous and forceful. Every sentence is either a question or a request or a demand. Did she not say of herself that she was sprung from 'a line of insatiable creatures'?

Her orders to artists, craftsmen, dealers show an artistic sensibility and an assured and individual taste. Several letters are directed to her cousin Niccoló da Correggio at Ferrara; he was a nephew of the great Borso d'Este. In fact, none was so well able to advise her as Niccoló, the very pattern of an accomplished Ferrarese courtier. He never missed a feast or a tournament. A fine judge of poetry and music, he was equally at home with the latest fashion, and himself designed jewellery and embroidery patterns.

Isabella's letters to her cousin quiver with curiosity and impatience. She envies other women's jewels and dresses even before they are worn, and she wants to read new books before publication. 'The more quickly these things reach us, the sooner and the more we shall appreciate them,' she wrote at nineteen.

She revelled in luxury. Launching new styles herself in hairdressing and clothes, she was often approached by the ladies of other courts requesting permission, in the most timid and respectful terms, to copy dresses created by the Marchioness of Mantua. When she was sixty, Francis I, King of France, asked her to send him a doll 'dressed like you, with the same sleeves, both inner and outer garments, with the same tiring of the head and dressing of the hair'.

The young Marchioness buys and buys and buys. Her infallible taste is a household word—who would dare to offer her a second-rate gem, or a pearl not of the first water? She refuses an emerald: 'The only emerald we will accept is one without cloudiness, and so beautiful that its match is not to be found in all the world.' She buys rubies, turquoises, coral, diamonds, pearls; she orders rings, buttons, belts, bracelets; she sends for magnificently worked silverware, Venetian crystal mirrors, iridescent glass from Murano.

But Mantua is not such a rich state as Ferrara; its lady gets into debt and often has to pawn her jewellery. A marchioness pledging her jewels? It is a common occurrence at this time. Her own brother Alfonso d'Este pledged the jewels of his wife Lucrezia Borgia to pay his war debts, did he not? And Pope Innocent VIII pawned his tiara for twenty thousand ducats.

Apart from the lady's outgoings, Francesco's warlike exploits swallowed up fabulous sums, and the state's deficit assumed threatening proportions. The Marquess tried to obtain a cardinal's hat for his brother Sigismondo, which came to seven thousand ducats, and so he pressed Isabella to throw her jewels into the scale. She fought back with her entire arsenal of feminine argument: 'Without jewels I should be forced to dress in brown, for if a woman of my rank were to show herself in brocade and coloured stuffs without jewels, she would be a laughing-stock.'

She overcome all financial obstacles and sacrificed all to the same one end: to make a great figure in the world. Her pages might sleep on straw, but at Court they were liveried in silk and cloth of gold.

A collector of objects of art, and a passionate one, was Isabella. Not a bankruptcy, not a sale, not an auction, but her agents were to be seen there, dealing, querying the price, haggling, running up the other bidders, even if these were there on behalf of the Doge or the Pope. Enthusiasm for the antique was general; a crowd of fanciers of classical art thronged about the excavations. Some of the competitors, such as Julius II, sometimes proved financially invincible; when in 1506 the

Laocoön group was dug up, the Pope acquired it, and Isabella had no choice but to have replica of it made.

Like all her contemporaries, Isabella loved clowns and dwarfs; like them, too, she delighted in cruel jokes. She dictated to her dwarf Matello anonymous letters addressed to courtiers, slanderous epistles composed only for the pleasure of angering the recipient.

Only in the perspective of her own time can we understand this strange alloy of rationalism and superstition: Isabella, a woman of remarkably clear intelligence, buys amulets favourable to one in childbed, snakes' tongues of magical power, lucky charms of silver. She writes in a letter: 'We wish to have one of those stones which make mushrooms come up in a single night.' She believes firmly in the efficacy of witches, magicians, demons and necromancers—just as many an Italian peasant does today.

Ludovico il Moro, Duke of Milan, one of the most brilliant princes of the Renaissance, had asked her hand in marriage. But too late. In 1491 he married her sister Beatrice. On that occasion Isabella did her utmost to appear at her most beautiful and elegant. Was she trying to eclipse her sister? Now and again an amorous tone is perceptible in her letters to Ludovico. In any case, gossip about their relationship had free rein.

The fall of Ludovico il Moro in 1499 in face of the military superiority of Louis XII put Isabella in a difficult situation. The French accused her of sympathy for the Sforzas, but Isabella was a mistress of stratagem. She quickly made an about-turn—not for nothing was she known as 'Macchiavelli in a skirt'—and in a letter to the French ambassador assured him that she was a 'buona francese'. But the Marquess too was a past-master of diplomatic ruses: sending gifts to the King of France, he granted him free passage and at the same time sent a letter which was a masterpiece of ambiguity to that arch-enemy of France, the Doge of Venice, in which he said: 'I am ready to throw myself into the arms of the Republic and sacrifice to it my possessions, my country, my soul. . . .'

It was with hardly contained repugnance that Isabella learned of the proposed marriage between her brother Alfonso d'Este and Lucrezia Borgia. What an unsuitable match! The future Lord of Ferrara, of the highest aristocratic descent, connected with all the greatest Italian families, to be joined in wedlock with the daughter of Alexander VI, that most unworthy pope! But this alliance being the wish of the King of France, she must bow to his decision.

We learn all the details of the wedding, down to the turnout of the ladies, together with Isabella's opinions on the subject, from her daily letters to her husband, who stayed behind at Mantua. Some of her biographers have seen fit to cite these letters as an example of feminine jealousy, since the criticism in them is often biting—but this is a mistake. No doubt Isabella did want her dresses to be more stylish than those of other ladies, and her retinue more sumptuously clad than that of Lucrezia. But certainly not out of personal vanity; she was leading an aesthetic mission, upholding the worth of her own principality. At this wedding Mantua must shine more brightly than Ferrara in the splendour of its representatives, but above all it must outshine Rome and the Borgias.

Isabella loathed Cesare Borgia, Lucrezia's brother, and yet she betrothed her son Federigo, future heir of Mantua, to Cesare's daughter when the boy was only two and the girl had not yet had her first birthday. (In fact the marriage never took place.) She stipulated the exact amount of dowry, writing unctuous letters to Cesare and telling him that this betrothal did great honour to her house and that thereby the marriage of their children would form an indestructible link between the Borgias and the Gonzagas—and all this though she hated and despised the Borgias. But then, as she was to write to her husband later, 'reason of state' must come first.

'Reason of state' was the mainspring of all politics at that day. Patriotism was a sentiment unknown to the Renaissance; collaboration with the enemy was the current coin. Just such opportunism prompted Francesco to offer his services to Louis XII when, in 1508, fortune seemed to favour France after the formation of the League of Cambrai, an alliance aimed against Venice. But the Venetian army counter-attacked, and the Marquess had the great misfortune of falling into their hands.

He bore his captivity hardly. Writing to Isabella, who had taken over the business of government, he is bitter, full of reproaches and even of jealousy, going so far as to accuse her of an affair with the marshal of the French diplomatic mission. It is not therefore surprising to find that he ends up by co-operating with the victor. He accepts the Doge's proposal to serve as *condottiere* of the Venetian forces.

Not that the Venetians trust him. How do they know he will not betray them again? Or go over to the enemy? Therefore they demand a precious hostage—none other than his son Federigo, at that time less than ten years of age.

Isabella revolts at that: 'He who takes Federigo from me takes my life!' But when the Pope intervenes with the suggestion of taking the boy under his protection, she yields. In July 1510 the Marquess is set free and goes to Rome with his son.

Sometimes in reading the letters of this pair we must ask ourselves what exactly was the relationship between husband and wife. What did they feel for each other? This mercenary general, entirely taken up with his military operations, how could he possibly feel at ease in the presence of such a brilliant wife, intellectually and even politically his superior? Indeed their married life was not without its anguish, its jealousies on one part or the other. The Marquess flaunts his mistresses, but Isabella, always the great lady, pretends to ignore them. Her letters to Francesco are full of gentleness and submission. One passage seems to reveal the nature of the link that bound them: 'The less love you show me, the more I shall love you, for this love is part of me. I was given to you so young that I cannot remember life without you.'

On one occasion only, Isabella lost her cool poise: hardly risen from childbed, she slapped a lady-in-waiting who was her husband's mistress. This was reported to the Marquess, who at the time was away from Mantua. Isabella apologizes, and offers to send a monk to negotiate a reconciliation. But Francesco replies: 'We wish neither monk nor priest . . know that we two are the marquisate of Mantua and apart from ourselves no one exists.'

The Marquess had been suffering from syphilis since 1512. When Isabella learned of this, which was at once, she withdrew from him, fearing even to take her meals at the same table. She travelled from city to city. Her visit to Rome in 1514, which even Pope Leo X tried to help her to protract by making pretexts, was to seem to her later like a beautiful dream. From Mantua she was to write to Cardinal Bibbiena: 'I am here in the body but I left my soul behind in Rome, talking to you without pause. . . .'

Many of her letters are shot through with a passionate

interest in aesthetic problems. No matter what the artistic or literary work, form and content are of equal importance to her; the plot of a play, its setting and scenery, a musical composition and the quality of the instruments which perform it; the content of a book and its binding.

So she becomes a bibliophile in the best sense of the term. Her letters to Aldus Manutius, the celebrated Venetian printer and publisher, reveal a whole chapter of the history of humanism. She has had a chance of admiring, while at Venice, the manificent volumes produced by Manutius. Now the printing press which has been in operation at Mantua for twenty years is not good enough for her. Herself a reader of Virgil, Livy and Pliny in the original, she commissions a small-format edition of these authors, to be printed on superfine parchment and bound in expensive leather. Of Petrarch, one of her favourite authors, she orders a manuscript copy to her own specifications. To this end she instructs an illuminator: 'Every word and every letter must be painted, not simply written.' Of course she will pay him, but only when the work is completed.

In fact, Isabella is spendthrift and miserly at the same time. When Manutius sends her his series of Latin authors in small format, each volume marked with the price as she had asked, she writes: 'Four of the little parchment volumes which you have sent are twice as dear as they should be, in the opinion of everyone at Court. We have returned them by your messenger.'

But modern authors of talent were also appreciated by the Marchioness; all but one, Pietro Aretino, an unscrupulous pamphleteer. She hated his calumnious and obscene writings, and showed her enmity in public. Later, when she was sixty, the spiteful and venemous Aretino described her as 'the monstrous Marchioness of Mantua, with teeth black as ebony, eyebrows white as ivory, unpardonably ugly and inexcusably painted'.

Ariosto had shown her, and to her alone, the original plan for his *Orlando Furioso*. Once more, as always, personal satisfaction was first in her mind. 'His visit was a delight to me,' she wrote her brother Alfonso d'Este, 'for he outlined for me the story of the poem he has devised. Thus we spent two whole days, which for me were not only free from vexation but full of enjoyment.'

The glorified picture of Isabella d'Este which the poets painted does not show us her true face. Though Ariosto lauds her in his thirteenth canto—*liberale e magnanima Isabella*—though other contemporaries crown her with laurels, the result is flavourless and stale. It is only by reading her letters that we can grasp the essentials of her character: her intellectual curiosity, her lucidity, her obstinate will. Objectivity is something to which she never gives a thought. Being the centre of a little world, she did not know, or wish to know, anything about its limits. It was she and she alone who counted. Every work of art might have been composed for her sole personal pleasure. Did it amuse me, or did it bore me? This is the only question she asks. And yet, in matters of poetry, or philosophic dissertation, or theological dispute, the judgment of Isabella still counts today as a critical touchstone, thanks to her vigorous personality. Even her vanity, her egocentricity, her worldly ambitions, were a stimulus to artists and men of letters, so that little by little her Court became one of the wittiest and most brilliant in all Italy.

Her husband died in 1519. Her son Federigo not yet being of age (he was only nineteen), Isabella became Regent of the Mantuan state.

She wanted above all things to get her second son Ercole elected cardinal. To this end she went to Rome, where she endeavoured to gain the favour of the Pope. But Clement VII turned a deaf ear. Two years later she went back, to live through days of terror. The troops of the Emperor Charles V, comprising German and Spanish mercenaries, got into the city, plundering and laying waste all that came in their path. From her window in the Palazzo Colonna Isabella could see soldiers dragging women into houses, throwing corpses out of the windows. All the horrors of the 'sack of Rome' took place before her eyes. The Ferrarese ambassador wrote from Rome: 'It cost the lady a superhuman effort not to give way to her nerves. The slaughter went on for days and days. The bloodthirsty soldiers once on the loose took no heed of their officers.'

But the Marchioness, under pressure from her followers to flee the city as soon as possible, stayed put. She stayed until the Pope, to whom she offered considerable sums, gave in and raised her son to the dignity of cardinal.

In order to keep an eye on the affairs of her sons Isabella employed every means, every stratagem. For instance she had certain documents stolen from the Vatican archives so that her son Federigo should not be involved in the fighting between the papal forces and those of the Emperor. But when she decreed the marriage of Federigo to Margherita Paleologa, Marchioness of Monferrato, complications ensued. Federigo was involved in a compromising situation with Boschetta, wife of the Count of Calvisano. Nevertheless the wedding took place. Isabella had the bride of her choice brought to Mantua, from which she had contrived to remove Boschetta.

That was her last diplomatic success. Now events took a different turn. Federigo, a clever intriguer, schemed against his mother to such purpose as finally to remove her from government. When he became Marquess, Isabella gave up the castle to him and took up her quarters in the upper floors of the Reggia, where her *Paradiso* was housed.

Thus exiled from power, Isabella d'Este took with her something that was to bring her a less tarnishable fame: her love of beauty and her vocation as a patroness of the arts.

PATRONESS OF THE ARTS

Isabella had these words engraved on a gem set in a trinket: *That I may live after my death.* At less than twenty years of age she was able to foresee the aura that would be created by and around her, in the light of eternity.

Always clear-headed about the purpose and consequences of her own actions, she protects the arts in the full consciousness of her mission. Royalty as she conceived it, the representative of a superior strain of human beings, puts one in mind of Nietzsche, who also glorified the tyrants of the Renaissance as protectors of culture.

Sometimes she loses touch with reality, and has the illusion that at a sign from her royal hand artists will bow to her will. But the times are marching on, and the social status of the artist is changing. Now it often happens more than once that the boot is on the other foot, so that the princes of this world wishing to display their power through some artistic medium, must ask the favour of the artist. To this Isabella will never consent.

We may imagine that a certain harmony may have obtained between her and Mantegna. They shared a love of the antique, and, more than that, the desire to combine such irreconcilable concepts as Christianity and paganism, earthly materialism and divine spirituality, and to weld these into an artistic whole.

Mantegna had been painter by appointment to the Gonzagas, until the day when Pope Innocent VIII summoned him to Rome. Three years later, in 1490, he returned to Mantua to complete his series 'The Triumph of Caesar', a triumph indeed in the antique manner. The series was completed about 1494. Six of the nine canvases were hung in the theatre hall of the castle, where they would do duty as a backcloth or cyclorama for classical plays (they are now at Hampton Court).

Since Mantegna's home was in Mantua, correspondence between him and Isabella would have been pointless. Hence we know little of their relationship. But among the artists working for Isabella, could he have been the only one not to suffer from her autocratic ways?

About the end of the century Isabella commissioned from Mantegna the pictures 'Parnassus' and 'The Triumph of Virtue over Vice', both now in the Louvre. Despite the too intellectual elaborateness of the subject, their beauty and delicacy endure. They graced her *studiolo* and were to serve as a guide to other painters.

At this period Isabella embarked on an extensive correspondence with artists living away from Mantua. Her letters are priceless as a source for her schemes, her tactics, her objectives.

No doubt it was no easy matter to satisfy her requirements. She chooses the subject, dictates the setting, summons the appropriate gods from Olympus and groups them on the stage; she casts this and that model for the parts of Chastity, Virtue, Vice and the rest. All is foreseen down to the finest detail. A start is made with a written synopsis, drawn up by Isabella alone or in partnership with some scholar. Then she has the cartoon or *scenario* roughed out by a draughtsman, always under her direction. She decides from what angle the picture shall be lit, and she adds a scale indicating height and width. While she shows a certain caution in dealing with important artists, she has no consideration for the others. The letters which she writes from Ferrara—at the age of eighteen—to Luca Liombeni, who was working on the decoration of her *studiolo*, are characteristic. 'If our *studiolo* is not finished by the time we arrive, we shall have you locked up in the dungeons of our castle.'

In another letter: 'Herewith a list of the devices which we wish to have painted on the frieze. On the inside of the cupboards you may paint according to your imagination, provided you have the right touch. We rely on your skill to dispose them to the best effect. If not, the painting will be done at your own charge and you will spend the winter in the dungeons. You may if you wish spend a night there now: that will give you some idea whether the lodging is likely to be to your taste.'

But what a change of tone in the letters commissioning some celebrity such as Leonardo da Vinci! The proud Marchioness would do anything to attract him. However, time and again Leonardo manages to avoid her orders, always producing some excuse. On 27th May 1501 Isabella asks a priest, Fra Pietro da Novellara, to intercede with Leonardo: 'Ask him if it would suit him to do a painting for our collection: if he consents, we leave the choice of date and subject to him. If he hesitates, at least try to persuade him to do us a little painting of the Madonna, pious and gentle, in his own manner.'

One month later Pietro da Novellara informs the Marchioness that Leonardo has not finished the pictures—'he is absorbed in the study of geometry'. A week after that, Novellara complains of the difficulty he is having in getting a painting out of Leonardo; he seems finally to have given the assurance that 'if he manages to come to terms with the King [of France] . . . then he will be free to serve Your Excellency with a better will than anyone in the world'. According to recent researches, Leonardo did paint a picture for Isabella in 1504 or thereabouts; it was 'Jesus and the Doctors'; it is now lost.

Being uncertain whether or not Leonardo would contribute something to her *studiolo*, Isabella tries to procure Perugino by the medium of Giovanna da Montefeltro, but is warned that Perugino is a slow and unsystematic worker. Isabella does not listen but writes to her agent Lorenzo da Pavia: 'It has lately been rumoured that Perugino is dead. If he lives, which is our hope, we pray you to ask him if he will do a painting for our *studiolo*.'

Negotiations with Perugino dragged on and on. It would take him five years to complete the order. Sometimes Isabella writes to him direct, sometimes she writes to friends to enlist their help. The archives contain no less than fifty-three such letters!

As always, she lays down the subject: 'My idea, which you

have to carry out, is to show the battle between Chastity and Love. Pallas Athene and Diana fighting Venus and Cupid. . . .'

Could it have been the licentious life of her husband that prompted Isabella to choose this austere Puritan theme? We could almost wish it so, for it would show a human and very feminine reaction.

The hundreds of pages written to Perugino are of unwonted exactness. She describes minutely the figures to be painted, both principals and supporting cast, even the details of their costumes. One of her letters ends thus: 'We send you, to round out our description, a little sketch for your better understanding. If you should find the group too crowded with characters, you may omit some of them, always provided that you retain the most important, that is, Athene, Diana, Venus and Cupid. But I forbid you to add figures according to your fancy.'

All the time Isabella keeps sending go-betweens to the studio of Perugino at Perugia, to check whether the artist is in fact working continuously and sticking to the schedule. But sometimes he promises to deliver the picture within a few days, sometimes the workshop is empty and the artist absent on some obscure business.

At last in June 1505 'The Triumph of Chastity', now in the Louvre, is finished, and in her hands: 'We have received the picture in flawless condition. We like it, both the design and the colouring.'

But there are worse complications with Giovanni Bellini. Here was a painter of subtle atmospheres. Would he bow to Isabella's purely intellectual *invenzione* or synopsis? He accepts the commission and with it an advance of twenty-five ducats, a quarter of the agreed fee. But some months later he becomes coy and suggests another subject: Madonna with Infant Jesus. Isabella accepts, though hesitantly, for this subject goes so badly with Mantena's allegories, but stipulates the addition of one other figure—that of St John, her husband's patron saint. Bellini rebels. Isabella's patience is at an end: 'We see clearly that the artist shows no respect for us. Not for one moment has he had any regard for our wishes, and we have resolved to recover the sum advanced.'

Bellini is now well over seventy years old, living at Venice, and is far from rich. In June 1504 he sends a picture, which is now lost, to Isabella. She writes back: 'The picture you have painted for us is worthy of your reputation. We shall overlook the lack of respect you have shown by the slowness of your work.'

But the *studiolo* is still not decorated throughout. Isabella is in touch with two artists, Lorenzo Costa and Francesco Francia, who share premises in Bologna. Costa's picture 'The Court of the Muses' is in the Louvre. It is perhaps the high peak of his creative work, with its untramelled composition, its unreal, fluid landscape. The figures are freely disposed, with the figure of Isabella dominating from the background. She is depersonalized, surrounded with allegorical characters. Who are they? The models were probably scholars, poets, musicians and ladies-in-waiting at Isabella's Court.

Francesco Francia was to paint her portrait. Isabella wrote: 'We do not wish the artist to come to our Court for this purpose. The last time our portrait was painted, we found the sitting still in one attitude so tedious that we do not wish to repeat. . . .'

Is this boredom the reason why there are so few portraits of Isabella? The only one drawn from the life and still extant is Leonardo's sketch (now in the Louvre), of which Lorenzo da Pavia wrote from Venice to the sitter: 'Leonardo da Vinci, who is at Venice, has showed me a portrait of Your Highness which is in all respects an exact likeness. Indeed it is so well done it could not be bettered.'

The portrait by Titian in the Vienna museum looks like the copy of a picture done by Francesco Francia from memory. It may be the one that Isabella mentions in a letter to Francia: 'Thanks to your talents you have painted us fairer than nature made us.' Is that a compliment to the artist, or a tactfully expressed criticism?

The second picture by Costa, also in the Louvre, may have been begun by Mantegna. It is a rather complicated allegorical composition, no doubt painted under Isabella's supervision. At this time Costa had already succeeded Mantegna as officially retained painter to the Mantuan Court.

Poor Mantegna! For more than half a century he had been in the service of the Gonzagas. 'An evil woman is three times more wicked than the Devil', Mantegna inscribed on his 'Samson and Delilah', now in the National Gallery, London, and which was painted at this time. Is this an allusion to Isabella's hardness of heart?

In January 1506 Mantegna, sick and oppressed by worry,

appealed to Isabella: 'I commend me to Your Grace since for weeks no one has paid me for my labours, and at this hour I am in the greatest distress . . .' and he offered her an antique marble bust for two hundred ducats.

There was no answer. Six months later Isabella sent an agent to Mantegna to try to get the bust more cheaply. Mantegna refused. The agent came back to borrow the bust so that his client could 'have a look at it'. The artist let him have the piece, but seemed very upset. 'I am persuaded almost,' writes the agent, 'that if he does not have his bust back within six days he will expire.'

Mantegna died on 13th September. Unmoved as always, Isabella wrote to her husband, who was then at Perugia: 'As Your Excellency had probably learned already, Signor Andrea died after your setting forth.' That is all—no word of regret.

And yet, even if her heart was never committed, her mind was always on the alert. She never let herself be contained by the manners of the past; she followed the evolution of art with curiosity and close attention. In 1521 she sent a young artist to Rome, to put himself in touch with new tendencies and to study at close quarters the work of Michelangelo and Raphael.

Rare are those who have such a sure and infallible taste for artistic values. Isabella d'Este remains the very incarnation of the Italian Renaissance, with all its dark cruelties and its dazzling sources of light.

CHAPTER THREE

POLITE SOCIETY

THE CURTAIN RISES

While woman was queen in Italy, how unhappy was the lot of women in France during the sixteenth century! All inveighed against them: poets, preachers, street-singers, all proclaimed the miseries of the wedded state, all spoke of those inferior beings who, under cover of simulated weakness, led man to evil. True, great lyric poets like Joachim du Bellay or Ronsard touched more delicate chords and were able to bestow a permanent value on the feeling of love. But what did these women themselves know of literature? The times were troubled by the Wars of Religion, outside the Court there was no cultivated society, and few women read. Neither Rabelais nor Calvin nor Montaigne wrote for women, besides which, remote from the Court, they were outside their sphere of influence.

Nevertheless there were princely circles in which ladies and gentlemen did meet for conversation. This is proved by Marguerite de Valois' *Heptameron.* The new element here is not the stories inspired by Boccaccio, it is the accurate observation from life. Lords and ladies discuss their amorous adventures reacting in an entirely personal manner, arguing, criticizing, laying bare their cases of conscience. The several 'dialogues on love' do not read like literature, but like the conversation of real life. Love is not sublimated here, and this is precisely the difference between this society and the polite society of the future. The women speak without restraint, not shunning crude expressions and indecent words. One of those present takes refuge in the higher spheres of amorous sentiment, quoting Plato. His companions retort: 'I believe, on my faith, that you have never been in love: else if you had felt its fire as others have, you would never talk of the *Republic* of Plato, who wrote but had no experience of life.'

Meanwhile, at Court, Italy comes into fashion. Translations

of Petrarch, Ariosto and Tasso appear, and the *Cortegiano* is much read. Poets, astrologers and preachers come from Italy in the train of Catherine de' Medici. The Court sets the whole country an example of good taste and refinement. As beauty is in Italy, so in France elegance is now the ideal.

Even outside the Court, with the improvement in material conditions, intellectual standards rise. The vein of erotic verse peters out; triviality is damped down, and mockery of women is a worn-out theme. New 'in-groups' are in search of an ideal; they are about to take up Platonism, expressed in the literary form of the pastoral.

This is best illustrated by the unrivalled success of Honoré d'Urfé's *L'Astrée*, the first volume of which came out about 1608. In this novel gallantry is pushed to the limits of refinement, a new society sees the fulfilment of its aims. Ladies and gentlemen see themselves reflected in these nymphs and shepherds and their innocent games of love. Celadon with his true love, the course of which runs roughly the length of five volumes until the moment when Astrée takes fire from his flame, is an example to every man in love.

Now begin the happy years when knowledge is to take pride of place over noble birth. This society, right at its beginning, brings into being the *honnête homme*, a phrase most inaccurately rendered by 'honest man'. More of a gentleman in the Victorian sense of that ideal—certainly not in the Elizabethan sense. A man of quality, indeed, but of mental and moral quality. A man of wit, not necessarily a witty man. He takes the place of the *cortegiano*; his manners are impeccable, his heart is noble, he is well-read but no pedant. He may be a commoner, but the social ladder is his to climb. His feminine counterpart is the great lady who sets the tone and whose mission it is to perfect society, polish its manners, mould its fashions. She defines the concept of moderation, limits excesses, but it must also be said that she curbs exuberant fancy and the artistic temperament.

Conversation, for which society exists, becomes an art, creates the style and permeates the written word. The metamorphosis of the spoken language into the written (or printed) language is complete. Now—and this is something new—men write for women to read. Furthermore, the new polite society aims to stand out from the crowd and if possible not to be understood by it. Thus metaphor and periphrasis are invented, obsolete words are banished, and the language is purged of expressions considered barbarous.

Philosophers appeal to a wider public, and do not write in Latin any more because women cannot read it. A clear and elastic style allows the lady of rank access to the upper reaches of science. Descartes frees philosophy of its scholastic trappings, Pascal theology from the dialectic of the Middle Ages.

We must not underrate the great influence of this new polite society. It created the form which allowed the French genius to take its flight to the higher spheres, and which will lead to greater things later on in the period of the classics. But their star will not shine brighter until these creative social forces have begun to dim.

MADAME DE RAMBOUILLET AND THE REIGN OF THE PRÉCIEUSES

Glory to the Marquise de Rambouillet: for hers was the first literary *salon*. The first French woman to direct affairs outside the royal circle, she reigned in her own *palais*, the Hôtel de Rambouillet. From her day onwards the *salons* of great ladies are to form a state within the State. How many more will imitate her outside the boundaries of France!

Little is known of her youth. Born at Rome in 1588, she was the only daughter of the French ambassador Jean de Vivonne, Marquis Pisani and his wife Giulia Savelli, of a Roman patrician family. In 1600, at the age of twelve, she was married to Charles d'Angennes, Marquis de Rambouillet. By 1610 she had already had seven children.

The only written sources available to biographers are first her letters to the wits who frequented her *salon*, and above all the *historiettes* written off the cuff about the middle of the century by her cousin Gédéon Tallemant des Réaux. A frequent guest in her *salon*, he knew all the regulars there, the great and the semi-great, and of course also the nibblers of literature, those who clipped its coins and picked the crumbs of its banquets. He is an amusing chatterer, but he has nothing to tell us of the spiritual and moral quality of his fellow-guests.

On her mother's side Madame de Rambouillet had Italian blood in her veins. Her childhood had been steeped in Italian civilization, marked by the reading of pastorals, of Tasso's *Aminta*, of Guarini's *Pastor Fido*. In Paris she took pleasure in reading Malherbe's odes and sonnets, admiring their tempered lyricism and elegantly manipulated language. But she found her life's ideal in *L'Astrée*. What a contrast to the atmosphere of the Court and its dissolute morals, which scandalized her: how much nobler was this world of *L'Astrée*, with its platonic ideas!

But can there really be such a society on earth? At least, this young noblewoman will try to create a society whose elegance and superior manners will not fall short of those current at the princely courts of Italy.

Her immediate aim is to set up a framework worthy of such a society. A town house in the Rue St-Thomas-du-Louvre had come to her in her dowry; it was in the very heart of Paris, and she had it pulled down. The plan of the house that was to take its place was the work of the owner herself, in all its details, the object being to obtain a series of reception rooms; the novelty was in the siting of the main staircase. Instead of occupying the centre of the building, as was then the fashion, it was to be built at one side of the main entrance hall. The façade of the huge rooms, lit by tall wide windows, gave on to the garden and was visible only to guests. These ideas were then so novel that the Regent Marie de' Medici is said to have brought her own architect's attention to that manner of building. The Hôtel de Rambouillet was finished about 1617.

The fashion of the day was for the lady of the house to receive her guests in a stateroom, in which the space between the bed and the wall was called the *ruelle*, and interviews in this gangway were denoted in the expression *tenir ruelle*. Red, and a ruddy brown, were the colours then in vogue for interior decoration, so the Marquise, inventive as ever, had her walls hung with blue brocade.

Here she is then, in her Blue Chamber, sitting on her state bed, surrounded by guests, model of a little world in the making: the world of polite society. In the background hovers a serious gentleman, taking hardly any part in the conversation; this is the Marquis de Rambouillet. When he finally died, hardly anyone missed him.

Her contemporaries say that the Marquise was as beautiful as she was virtuous, as attractive as she was inaccessible. Voiture writes: 'There never was a lady who understood gallantry so well, and gallants so badly.' Malherbe had made an anagram on her name, Catherine: it was Arthénice. Under it, he wrote poems to and about her. He makes no secret of having loved her without hope, when he says that, on fire with love for a heart of ice, he had to quench the flames.

Such was Arthénice. She encouraged friendship but never had an affair. Only thus could she re-create the fashionable Arcady of *L'Astrée*, where shepherds for ever languished at the feet of modest nymphs; only thus could she conjure up the image of the distinguished person and endow it with aesthetic values. For to be distinguished implied much more than having an aristocratic outlook; it meant distilling one's feelings into a graceful and nicely regulated scale of shades of expression. Thus one became one of the *précieuses*: and preciosity was a virtue.

The now vanished art of conversation was launched by the Marquise. Much more highly esteemed than gambling or dancing, it became the aim of society and the reason for its existence. Not gossip about love affairs, such as was to be heard at Court. Of course, in the *salon* the news of the day at Court and about town are mentioned, feelings of love are analysed, motives are plumbed; but these highly psychological conversations, which devise a metaphysical system for love, explore refinements in the relationship of man to woman. For all we know, the *précieuses* may not have lacked for amorous adventure; in their private lives they may have had no leanings at all towards sublimated love. But in the Rambouillet *salon* their wish is to crown themselves with a halo as of an inaccessible goddess. The only love they recognize is a pure and platonic one, and they repudiate all vulgar passion. Innocence comes into fashion, and the *jeune fille naïve*, the innocent young girl, makes her bow in literature under the auspices of the *Chambre bleue*.

From time to time a newcomer, ignorant of the usages of polite speech, dares to utter a badly constructed sentence or a too-ordinary word. Veiled glances are exchanged, there is some dry coughing, smiles hidden behind fans. These people are soaring above the level of earthly life, they walk in supra-terrestrial spheres.

The Marquise however is no pedant. She knows just how to transform gossip into conversation of general interest and how to attune it to a higher plane. As she is so fond of saying, daily life must be *debrutalized*. She is not exactly prudish, but indecency is barred. Her cousin Tallemant des Réaux declares, 'One would not dare utter the word arse.'

She is against intrigue; this is part of her integrity of character. Father Joseph, the Grey Eminence of Richelieu, had told her that the all-powerful Cardinal might show favour to her husband, if only she would keep him supplied with current gossip about the love affairs of certain prominent people. She refused coldly, saying that spying was not in her line. 'How happy I am,' she added, 'not to be living at Rome, where rumour might have linked my name with that of some cardinal!'

In her family life there were many trials to put up with. Two of her children died in infancy, three of her daughters taking the veil. Only her son, the Marquis Pisani, and her daughter Julie stayed on at the Hôtel to represent the younger generation. But the son was to fall on the field of battle at the age of thirty. His mother withstood this buffet of fate like the great lady she was, without giving a sign of bitterness or disappointment, or voicing her inner thoughts.

Julie, youngest of the *précieuses*, was also one of the most accomplished; witty, cultivated, distinguished, virtuous, she had no use for marriage. In which she resembled her mother, who was wont to say, 'If I had not been the victim of convention I should never have married.' Like her mother too, Julie eschewed all love affairs. She was indignant when Voiture tried to brush her arm with his lips. This gave him a splendid opportunity to turn some commonplace verses!

Julie was beautiful, and the Marquis de Montausier was not unmoved by her virtues. From their first meeting he was madly in love with her, but she kept this faithful Celadon waiting for fourteen years. In hopes of moving her, he went off to the wars. He addressed impassioned declarations to her; and in 1641 he hired several poets to compose the famous *Garland for Julie*, a masterpiece of calligraphy and floral illumination, as the apotheosis of his beloved. But still Julie was unmoved, even when the Queen Mother and Mazarin intervened in Montausier's favour. She was only to yield at the age of thirty-eight, when the marriage at last took place. But the long waiting had only served to embitter Montausier, which is not surprising, and it is suspected that he served as the model for Moliere's *Misanthrope*.

To us in our day the sickly flattery that surrounded Julie and her friend Angélique Paulet seems childish if not ridiculous.

Now Angélique is 'the fair lioness', because of her auburn hair; now the poets see her as an inaccessible nymph, turning into a fierce lioness in the fury of her frigidity. Again, she will figure as a diamond resistant even to fire. The allegories of *L'Astrée*, it is plain, are an unconscionable time a-dying. Like ghosts they permeate the atmosphere of the times.

Although the Marquise de Rambouillet reigned over a little literary kingdom she wrote nothing herself. And if she wrote letters, which we may well suppose, nothing of them has come down to us. She confesses, 'I have no acquaintance with the Muses.' But were they entirely missing from her life? Did she never feel real emotion even on reading a poem? Literature, we must admit, was for her simply a means of presenting men with the ideal of beauty, to help them transmute feeling and thought into harmonious forms.

In her Blue Chamber guests of the most various origin rubbed shoulders: writers, wits, citizens, divines, ladies of high birth. There were to be found the great Condé, then still Duc d'Enghien, Richelieu, the Duchesse de Longueville, the Duchesse de Ghevreuse, Rotrou, the Scarrons, husband and wife, Ménage, Mairet, Georges de Scudéry, and his sister. La Rochefoucauld came in 1631, when he was eighteen; and in 1654, for the first time, Madame de Sévigné at a very tender age.

The Blue Chamber becomes the tabernacle of literature. Writers, both the dedicated and the beginners, attend it, filled with a sense of mission, laden with manuscripts in folio, in quarto, in octavo, from which they read aloud, both their own and others' work. The guests listen respectfully, for listening has become one of the polite arts. These readings are truly ceremonious. The carefully polished phrases, the disciplined style, lightly peppered with Italian words; the commentary on recently issued works; the mutual compliments; exposition of a phrase; discussion round some grammatical problem; and from time to time some critical insight—it all gives the opportunity to display one's verbal dexterity.

Of course this society lacked the solid foundation of tradition. Everything had to be built and shaped. But the hostess herself conferred on it a style which was to endure for more than a hundred years. Thanks to her, the conception of an intellectual *élite* was born, which is something that cannot be too highly valued.

There are times when men arise to lead revolt and unrest. By contrast, in this first third of the seventeenth century, the *honnêtes gens* diffused calmness and deliberation. Their very virtues may seem tedious to us today, but in the light of the age which had just passed, with its discord and social cleavage, calm wisdom appeared as a novelty quite as intoxicating as any revolutionary ferment with its drums and trumpets.

We watch the outward life of men and women in this society; but how shall we perceive their state of mind? Living as we do in an age when all the classic rules of art and poetry have been broken, what sympathy can we have with a society which had for its purpose the quest of form?

For the ladies of the Rambouillet household, the old poet Malherbe represented the new ideal. He ruled as Master of the Blue Chamber down to his death in 1628. It was he who had given power to conversation, measure to verse, grace to the sonnet; by him the language was purged of exotic words, and poetry of all truculence. He never admitted the slightest poetic licence, but always sacrificed subjective feeling to impeccable grammatical form. The Marquise knew very well why she had made him the magnetic pole of her *salon*; she recognized in him the mind most able to give her circle a groundwork of order and discipline, without which the polite society could not be attained.

But there were certain dangers inherent in the mastery of a poet like Malherbe over the tone of this *salon*. The avoidance of all emotion, of all spontaneity, bore in itself the seeds of formalism. Thus writers like Guez de Balzac, Voiture and Chapelain, who after Malherbe's death succeeded him in the Blue Chamber, were typical of the literature of their time, but all authors of the second rank.

From 1625 onwards, Voiture never missed the daily dinner. Voltaire wrote of him in 1752: 'Voiture, whose native genius was frivolous and facile, was the first to shine in that dawn of French literature. If he had come after the great men who adorned the century of Louis XIV, he would have had to show more than wit.' What was good enough for the Hôtel de Rambouillet was not good enough for posterity.

In other pages of his work Voltaire cries down the Rambouillet establishment. However, we consider his verdict too severe: Voiture was well-read, had quite wide acquaintance with literature, and this means a great deal when we consider the low educational standards of his age. At the beginning of the century it was still no rarity to encounter a gentleman who could not read or write. Of course today when we read his tame and flavourless poetry we find it hard to understand the status he enjoyed with the contemporary reading public. But one must take into account that he wrote for, and spoke exclusively to, the closed circle of the Hôtel de Rambouillet, where every occasional verse from his pen and every point that he made in conversation thrilled someone. His ascent to the status of literary star proves how indifferent that society was to the accident of birth, for he was the son of a wine-merchant. A pert little man, he knew how to make his weight tell by his accomplished bearing, his liveliness, prompt repartee, his nicely calculated effects. Ladies, too, appreciated his gift as a riddle-master and master of the revels: for in their set, gaiety was the order of the day; not a hint of trouble or of family misfortunes was allowed to break the surface in this brand-new society, already so self-assured.

The most perfect mirror of these times is to be found in letters rather than in general literature, which tends to be abstract, given to histrionics and allegory. The correspondence between Voiture and his friend and rival Guez de Balzac is an example. As in a reflection of the *salon* conversation, we see the characters as in life and hear them trading compliments, uttering their civil and never malicious observations, their delicate mockery. 'You are the parent of the noble style,' writes Voiture to Balzac —but he may have smiled as he wrote the words. Balzac is the model of preciosity (which at this time, we repeat, was a virtue). One would think that he had devoted his entire life to the improvement of his writing style. He ushered in the era of letter-writing that was to flourish for the next two centuries. Later on he was to be decried as a mere maker of phrases, but polite society owed him much. He composed a digest of Greek and Latin literature for ladies. He wrote: 'I made learning accessible and I showed the way to many.' Such great minds as Bossuet and Pascal were to make good use of the 'noble style' which he invented.

The home of this 'noble style', the Hôtel de Rambouillet, was nothing less than the forerunner of the Académie Française, created in 1634 and likewise dedicated to the reform of language. Indeed, some of the brightest stars of that *salon*, Voiture, Balzac,

Chapelain and Vaugelas the grammarian, were among the founding Academicians.

Chapelain, who first broached the project of the famous dictionary, had taken Malherbe's place in the Blue Chamber. His conversation was so copious and elegant that ladies brought a blind eye to bear on his untidy clothes and dirty wig. His critical pronouncements caused a sensation. Never up to that time had literary works been assessed *sub specie aeternitatis*; people delighted in elaborate metaphor, in moving perorations, and the only faults that came under fire were those of grammar and style. Chapelain introduced a new element; a literary criticism much like our own, an attempt to distinguish between what is of worth and what is not. But it is interesting to learn that ladies, more or less amateur readers, were better equipped with critical instinct that Chapelain, the dedicated professional. When the *Discours de la Méthode* came out in 1637, the *précieuses* greeted it with enthusiasm. They could do no other than claim Cartesianism for their own, preaching as it did the supremacy of Reason, regarding Beauty and Truth as one. How could they see Descartes as anything else but an incarnation of the genius of the times? But Chapelain demurs: Descartes' theories, he says, lack proof, and lead to false conclusions. The seed of doubt is sown, already dividing society into two factions.

Controversy about problems of the stage is even more passionate. At this time, it is unthinkable that the Marquise and her ladies should mingle with the rowdy public in the pit of the Hôtel de Bourgogne. New plays are read and discussed in her own *salon*. Argument about the rule of the three unities lasts late into the night, the ladies refusing to admit the propriety of changing a few items of scenery to represent respectively a palace, a battlefield, a forest. . . . How can one assume that some years have passed in the space of a few hours? . . . And they greet with satisfaction the new revelation of the Aristotelian rule about unity of time, place and action.

Once more society is threatened with rigidity. Corneille has transgressed the rules of unity. But is there any awareness in the Blue Chamber that a new immortal work has been born in *Le Cid*? Keen minds quibble about its faults. Georges de Scudéry, pretentious and jealous, stirs up the famous *querelle du Cid* in the hope that unfavourable criticism will somehow react to the advantage of his own plays. The plot of *Le Cid* he says, is worthless, the verse is bad, the rules are disregarded. The Academy takes up the quarrel, and the opinion of the *précieuses* is divided. Richelieu, himself the author of bad plays, takes sides with Scudéry. To do her justice, we must record that the Marquise sided with Corneille.

What great dramatists were to be seen at her *salon*? All of them, according to the Rambouillet lobby of historians, but in fact this flat assertion is not supported by written evidence. One thing is certain: in 1643 Corneille read his *Polyeucte* there, for the first time. But what a disappointment for the author! The reception was icy, his audience finding the Christian sentiments too high-flown and with too much Jansenist rigour. This is characteristic of their taste; they go to mass, they have their confessors, their spiritual directors, but they refuse to be blindly devout. It is a part of good breeding to be religious in a measure half-way between Christian virtue and Socratic wisdom.

Little by little, jealousy makes itself felt at Court. The *précieux* are mocked, called the lazy ones because unlike courtiers they take no part in political intrigue and plot. Madame de Motteville, a lady-in-waiting, writes in her memoirs that fear of the verdicts of the Hôtel de Rambouillet grew steadily at Court. This fear was not unjustifiable, for here for the first time a new phenomenon, hereafter to be called Public Opinion, is born. The Court, scenting danger to the monarchic principle, makes a virtue of inquiring into the political tone of the *salons*. Richelieu sends an emissary, the Abbé Boisrobert, to the Marquise to look into the opinions of her regular guests. But she shows diplomatic ability. 'The people who come here are so well aware of the high opinion I hold of His Eminence that not one of them would have the boldness to speak ill of him in my presence.'

Around the middle of the century the great age of the Hôtel de Rambouillet had run its course. Its ageing mistress—she was to die in 1665—is no longer the ruling queen of the literary world. Moreover, the Fronde has given rise to feelings of insecurity in society. Nevertheless, the Marquise has set an example to many imitators; there is always someone new beginning to *tenir ruelle*. Madame de Sablé has a *salon* in which are framed not so much critical judgements but opinions of more general application. From these La Rochefoucauld is to draw material for his *Maximes*. Madame de Longueville, Madame de Maure, Madame Scarron who is to become Madame de

Maintenon—all these surround themselves with their circle of intellectuals.

The very concept of preciosity—today a term of disparagement—broadens out to comprise urbanity, wit, or a state of mind. The word preciosity, or rather its equivalent, *préciosité*, passes into general use and acquires many meanings: thus Madame de Sévigné in one of her letters speaks of the preciosity of her long widowhood. Books are published, as for instance the *Dictionnaire des Précieuses* in 1660, edited by Somaize. Many expressions drawn from their familiar speech pass into the language and stay there. The *précieuses* form themselves into social sets, mocked by Molière, described with irony by La Fontaine, and the subject of rhymes like this by Boileau.

Dull authors to their parlours oft repair
By readers scorned, to find some solace there.

MADEMOISELLE DE SCUDÉRY

Mademoiselle de Scudéry lived through the great days of 'precious' society: she also witnessed its decadence. Consistent in her attendance at its congregation, the Hôtel de Rambouillet, it was there that she came to recognize the omnipotence of letters, and there she was initiated into the secrets of literary creation.

Coming of ancient and noble stock, it may be that she sought to express her pride of lineage in the novel. The fruits of her labours were abundant; first *Cyrus the Great* in ten volumes, published between 1649 and 1653, each volume running to a thousand pages.

This was the best-seller of the mid century, and was translated into German, Italian, English, Spanish, and even into Arabic, to the profit of sundry publishers if not of the author. To us in our day the immense success of this exclamatory novel seems inconceivable. But we must take into account that this was a *roman à clef*, stuffed with disguised contemporary gossip, a mirror indeed of polite society. And the same society saw itself here explained and magnified, finding in its pages many a recipe for gracious living.

The leading characters are very easy to identify. The Hôtel de

Rambouillet appears under the name of Hotel de Cléomire. And Cléomire is none other than the Marquise, of whom the author says, 'Her intellect is not one of those that function only by the light of nature, for she has cultivated it with great pains . . .'—the ultimate in praise, for a *précieuse*. Cyrus (the Prince de Condé) loves Mandane (Madame de Longueville). All ends well, but before this inevitable happy ending there are many enemies to overcome. The solution, which was made as a concession to the readers' susceptibilities, did not suit the taste of Mademoiselle de Scudéry, for whom renunciation constituted the supreme virtue. 'It is almost as necessary,' she wrote, 'to be unhappy as to be in love.' The resigned hero is glorified in *La Princesse de Clèves* as in the tragedies of Racine. And even Saint-Evremond was to exclaim: 'Langour in love is the most delicate act, it is a flame that consumes love!', but that was later, when delicacy was even more prized than politeness.

As for Mademoiselle de Scudéry herself, she draws her own portrait in *Cyrus the Great* under the name of Sapho, which is to remain a favourite one in 'precious' circles. 'Sapho is not beautiful, yet she is able to inspire greater passions than the greatest beauties on earth.' Her friends, no doubt understanding the allusion to her Celadon's love, might well smile on reading this phrase: for it was well known that for many long years Pellisson, the historian of the Academy, and the ugliest man of the century according to a contemporary, had been madly in love with her.

Some years later she published another book, *Clélie*, a kind of *ars amandi* for inexperienced youth. Its second volume contains the famous Chart of the Emotions, with its Geography of Love; at first this item was all the rage but later it was mocked and even parodied. The characters in 'Cyrus' were Persians, those in *Clélie* were Romans, and their actions were motivated by heroism in the antique manner. But their speech is straight out of the repertory of 'precious' gallantry, a faithful record of the elegant dialogue that was to be heard in the Rambouillet *salon*.

This elegant construction was bound to be demolished sooner or later. Boileau undertook the housebreaking. He wrote: 'It is a great absurdity in this lady to have written this work and chosen the most serious age of the Roman Republic as a background for portraits of French people of our day.' The authoress took her revenge by scheming against the admission of Boileau to the Academy.

Madame de Sévigné's letters are not lacking in spiteful little allusions to the novels of Mademoiselle de Scudéry. However, since for many years she moved in 'precious' circles, it is there that she learnt to communicate her ideas and to express herself with taste and refinement. But compare her letters, so full of sap and shimmering colours, easy and delicate, psychologically subtle, with the bulky literary products in vogue at Hôtel de Rambouillet, and you will see that she has outclassed her instructors. Finally, Madame de La Fayette too came from the same circle which handed on to her that purity of style and quest of perfection which are sublimated in her immortal novel *La Princesse de Clèves*.

About the middle of the century Mademoiselle de Scudéry began to keep a *salon*: this was the beginning of her famous Saturday at-homes, which became famous but were also much decried. A miserably thin little woman, with no trace of flirtation 'very ugly in part' as Chapelain said, Mademoiselle de Scudéry opted out of all competition in the field of feminine coquetry. On the other hand, she had no equal as the very spirit of preciosity. Fine phrases and the glorification of virtue ever reigned supreme in her house, where everyone expressed themselves in high-flown orotund language, like the dialogue in her novels.

One thing counterbalances this excess of virtue, and soon Mademoiselle de Scudéry is to give it form by inventing the written 'portrait'. Those present, and more especially those absent, are analysed, dissected, stripped of their artificial mask; their character laid bare, their secret motives revealed. A dangerous game indeed. It sows discord, sunders old friendships, lets the seed of hatred germinate. Since many authors go to the Saturday at-homes, this spiteful game sets its mark on their work. It is no mere chance that at this very time letters and memoirs are crammed with sneaking analysis, wounding psychology.

In the heyday of the Hôtel de Rambouillet people wrote as they spoke; in the day of its decline they spoke as they wrote; more and more elaborately, artificially, exaggeratedly. Now indeed we may equate preciosity with affectation. What was once boundless urbanity changes into sheer convention. Wit is over-distilled and the bogey of pedantry threatens. Boileau with his satires, La Rochefoucauld with his biting aphorisms, Molière with his mockery will bring down this fabric so solidly built.

THE PRÉCIEUSES ON THE STAGE

The first performance of *Les Précieuses ridicules* was on 18th November 1659 at the Petit-Bourbon theatre. The scene is laid in the house of a citizen of Paris. The party of Mascarille, a footman posing as a marquis, was played by Molière himself. The two heroines, Cathos and Madelon, were played by actresses in a marked Italian or Spanish accent, because it was the fashion of the *précieuses* to speak French in this way (thus for instance sounding all the 'e's which in proper French are mute).

All Paris—the Court, the nobility, even to the aged Marquise de Rambouillet, was in the audience. Was Mademoiselle de Scudéry there? History does not record. But the play must have been a blow to her pride, for the two young ladies from the country had borrowed their entire vocabulary from *Cyrus the Great* and learnt their Geography of Love from the Chart of the Emotions. And when Madelon says: 'I vow I dote on Portraits, there is nothing to my mind so smart . . .' this can only be an allusion to the favourite parlour-game of the Saturday at-homes.

It is a success; laughter comes from all parts of the house. The aristocrats laugh at the citizens who are at such pains to put on airs and cannot tell a real marquis from a bogus one; the ladies of Paris laugh at country girls imitating them; and the old Marquise too shares the general hilarity, for here the target of mockery is not the true *préciosité* but the abuse of it. But malicious tongues whisper: Cathos? Is not the Marquise Catherine by her Christian name? And Madelon? Madeleine de Scudéry? . . .

Never mind that, preciosity will be discredited, its *salons* will be the target of mockery. It is all very well for Molière to write in the preface of his comedy: 'The true *précieuses* would be wrong to take offence at a play which shows their clumsy imitators.' It is too late, their reign has run its course.

Louis XIV commissioned Molière's company to act the play at Court. What a delight it was to hear that mockery of the *salons* in which, according to rumours that had come to his ears, an opposition to his total power was brewing! Henceforward he will supplant them by taking the reins of literature into his own hands, by patronizing such authors as Molière and Racine, by being in the phrase of the day, their shield and sword against their enemies. The glory of these two, as of Bossuet and Boileau, will shed its light on the King and imbue him with that lustre which will lead Voltaire to call his age 'the century of Louis XIV'.

NINON DE LENCLOS

'These precious ladies,' exclaimed Ninon de Lenclos, 'are the Jansenists of love.' This sounded like a jibe, but like all her jibes it went to the heart of the matter. The *précieuses* make war on free love as the Jansenists make war on free thought. The orthodoxy of both sects is equally austere, rigorous, moralizing. Ninon, on the other hand, moved in an atmosphere of gaiety. Religious dogma and platonic love alike were foreign to her. There is no place in her philosophy for transcendental values.

Three centuries have gone by to tarnish her image. Down to our own day biographers avid for sensation have gone to the pages of Tallemant des Réaux, who knew her well, admittedly, but whose *Historiettes* turn the spotlight on her amorous adventures in one anecdote after another. Each of his successors added something spicy of his own brewing, until finally Ninon has become a novelette heroine, who thanks to her unageing freshness has afforded ideal advertising matter for the Fountain of Eternal Youth.

But the true Ninon is no such dubious personality. A typical figure of enlightened society, already touched by the charm of the eighteenth century, she holds all the vigour of the Great Century. To our eyes she is like a picture in which two styles mingle, in one amalgam of timeless poetry, to which her emotional life forms a fragile and exquisite frame. The very spirit of her times shines out from her. Those graces which she has received she dispenses to her surroundings with a boundlessly generous hand.

Portraits of Ninon, dressed in the solemn fashion of the times, like that attributed to Mignard, match ill with the idea we have formed of her. We should like to see her less majestic, more arcadian, haloed in lace and a froth of muslin, a star among the beauties which crowd the barque for Cythera.

For all its formalism and ceremony, how free of prejudice was this society, compared with that of the bourgeois nineteenth century! Any retired prostitute, once she was living on the increase of her savings and not on her night-to-night earnings, and provided she was literate and had presentable manners, would have access to the best society. This Ninon foresaw instinctively; as early as the period of her 'working' life she had taken advantage of her charms to choose lovers among men of solid worth, making friends of them for life. The friendship which bound her to Saint-Evremond, one of the most original characters of the period, is typical of her flair for quality. He had what it took to please her: wit, scepticism, freedom of imagination. For the rest of his life after he had fled to England—he died in 1703—Ninon kept up a warm correspondence with him that lasted forty years.

In 1650, when Ninon was thirty, her friends exclaimed: 'Ninon's affections are steady—she must be growing old.' The truth was that she had found her first love in the Marquis de Villarceaux, a handsome man by whom she had a child. The affair lasted for three years, which by comparison with past unions (and with those to come) was an eternity.

To be sure, there was no great pressure of prejudice in matters of love at this period; but in the case of religious obedience it was far otherwise. And in this field Ninon had given such open proof of slackness that the Regent, Anne of Austria, sent her to the Madelonnette. All Paris was moved by it. Was it possible? Ninon, the gracious, the accomplished, the adorable Ninon, in a convent appointed for the reform of sinners? Personalities in high places intervened, procuring her transfer to a smarter convent. Here she received many visitors: even Christina of Sweden came to see her and enjoy her sprightly conversation.

The incarceration was not to last long: only eight months. After which she took up a life which we can almost describe as middle-class, soon becoming known no longer as Ninon but as Mademoiselle de Lenclos. A canny investor, she was able to live on her dividends, which were not very large, but then she lived on a modest scale. In 1678 she bought a small town house in the Rue de Tournelles, near the aristocratic Place Royale, which is now the Place des Vosges.

Her friends the Scarrons lived quite near: Scarron as a writer, was not a member of the *précieux* circle. On the contrary, everything that came from the pen of this ugly and insincere man, who wrote the *Roman comique*, is malicious, vulgar, if not obscene, every word a blow struck at the spirit of polite society. He had married Françoise d'Aubigné, his junior by twenty-five years. They formed an ill-assorted couple indeed, but this surprised nobody. She was an orphan born in prison, with no home and no one to love her, and at sixteen years of age had taken refuge with this misshapen creature. There was plenty of gossip about her private life, including her friendship with Ninon. Did Ninon really hand on Villarceaux, the love of her life, to Françoise? Fifty years later she answered this among the other indiscreet questions of Saint-Evremond: 'I know nothing, I saw nothing. I simply lent my yellow room to her—and to Villarceaux—often.' Certainly no one in daily contact with Françoise, so flirtatious and casual, would have seen in her the future Marquise, still less the bigot inciting the King to clericalism and intolerance. But once Marquise de Maintenon, and in the end wife to the King, she tried to wipe out her past, and came to visit Ninon only in secret.

In the 1660s, when the Hôtel de Rambouillet was living on its past glories, a new day dawned for the *salon* of Ninon. Older now, she finds herself surrounded with respect—a whole society in the process of evolution resorts to her *salon*, as to a veritable Elysium of free thought. Preciosity has given way to salty repartee, and the intelligentsia is off in search of new adventures. Subjects of conversation, far from being frivolous, revolve round a new kind of wisdom, a philosophy that we might call existentialist. For the first time the fabric of faith, for all its solid foundations, is severely shaken. The precepts of religion are no longer blindly followed, but compared with the laws of nature, with reason and with knowledge.

The newcomers to the philosophy abstain, for the moment, from all ideological propaganda. Without openly proclaiming their liberal ideas, they just touch on major problems in a tone that is meant to be playful. Above all nothing, not the slightest echo, must be heard at Versailles. Nobody is anxious to share the fate of Saint-Evremond, who paid for his boldness with exile for life.

In Ninon's Arcady there meet people whose scratches draw

no blood, whose scepticism overthrows no principle, and who, for the moment at least, veil themselves in discreet smartness.

Ninon's favourite reading is still Montaigne; his essays remain her bedside book. Montaigne has taught her to look on traditional values with a critical eye, opening the way for her towards an epicurean optimism which offers an escape from her own troubles as well as those of other people, and is opposed to intolerance and to pride. Ninon is exceptionally independent of mind, receptive to all that complements her true being, rejecting all that is contrary to her nature. She is clever at juggling with quotations from standard authors, but forgets what they meant originally and confers an entirely new meaning on them. Her admirers claim that perhaps she manufactured them herself throughout. She herself says, 'I can profit by all the freedom of ignorance.'

The Princess Palatine, a born rebel, among her trenchant criticisms of people and their failings, appreciated Ninon none the less: 'there is no more *honnête homme* than Ninon'. And Saint-Simon, otherwise pitiless and mordant, writes thus of her *salon*:

'Everything that took place in her house did so with a respect and outward decency such as high-born princesses rarely attain. All was there delicacy, lightness, measure, and went to make up a conversation that she kept up by her wit, and by her store of factual knowledge of all the ages. The extraordinary respect which she had acquired, the number and distinction of her friends and acquaintances, endured after her charms had ceased to attract people to her.'

Nevertheless there were not wanting those who cried down Ninon's *salon*. They were to be found mostly in clerical circles, among those who feared in the rise of scepticism the decay of their power. More than once they sent their scouts to sound out opinion in Ninon's house, seeking ammunition in their struggle against free thought. But Ninon had a short way to unmask hypocrites and sent them about their business.

Her friendship with Molière began in 1661 or thereabouts, and arose out of the numerous characteristics they shared: an aversion from prudishness and false learning, openness of mind and generosity of heart. That is why she was the first to hear him read his *Tartuffe*—in 1664. Tartuffe is the very symbol of deceit, the immortal personification of hypocrisy, a bitter joke against bigotry and narrow-mindedness, whose comedy is already soaked in the spirit that Ninon and La Rochefoucauld and the Prince de Condé represent. She is to support Molière in his struggle against the pious, who are still powerful enough to prevent the performance of this masterly comedy for five years.

The most fashionable thing in Paris is to be received at Ninon's. There one meets high society, but also the more gifted of the *précieuses*, such as Mademoiselle de Scudéry, who feel at home there. The beautiful Madame de la Sablière, a friend of Ninon's, keeps a *salon* too, patronizing authors of note, especially La Fontaine, who finally takes up his quarters with her. It is here that Ninon meets Boileau, whom she is to protect against the attacks of the theological faculty, that enemy of cartesianism.

At Madame de la Sablière's, about the end of 1672, a supper is held at which the outlines of an imperishable work take shape. Ninon is present among others who include Boileau, Molière, La Fontaine. Molière outlines his plan for *Le Malade imaginaire*, intended to denounce the pretensions of ignorant quacks. He reads out some of the scenes he has finished. Very luckily for posterity a doctor, François Bernier, is among those present. From the light of his own experience he recalls the various stages of medical study, the absurd questions discussed in theses, the grotesque ceremonies of graduation, the dog-Latin of consultations. Amid general hilarity the fever mounts. Those present contribute to an improvised performance, and so, conducted by Molière, the third intermezzo of the *Malade imaginaire*, with its parody of ridiculous graduation ceremonies, a masterpiece of burlesque, is born to strike a mortal blow to charlatanism.

At this time Ninon reached the zenith of her brilliance, so that Saint-Evremond could write to her: 'I hold you to be the happiest creature that ever was, now in the prime of life as you are.' She has by no means given up her amorous adventures, her caprices as she calls them, the fruit of passing fancies. In 1671, being then fifty-one years of age, she figures thus in a letter from Madame de Sévigné to her daughter: 'Your brother is under the spell of Ninon. I doubt if it will be good for him. There are those to whom it has done no good; she quite spoiled your father.' But when Ninon spurned the young marquis, his mother was offended: 'The other day Ninon was saying to my son that he had a heart like pumpkin mixed with snow, a soul of broth, and a body of wet paper!'

However, twenty years later Madame de Sévigné wrote that a friend 'reports on the marvellous good company he finds at Mademoiselle de Lenclos's; everything there puts one in mind of the old days, herself and the men and the women.'

Endowed with a highly original personality, Ninon always moved with the times; her conversation was never behind the fashion, as so often happened with the *précieuses*, because she never stopped exploring new ground. The Abbé de Châteauneuf, said to have been her last lover, boasted of her lively taste in music. Lully, anyhow, was a frequent guest in her house, where the partisans of the old and the new styles in music confronted each other. At the outset of the new century, when the public was surfeited with opera, Ninon too rose up against the prevalent 'false taste'. Let the Abbé de Châteauneuf report some things she said in 1705, the very year of her death: 'Instead of keeping music for solemn occasions or for intermezzos in Molière's plays, they now have the idea of setting a whole tragedy to song from beginning to end, down to the most commonplace recitative.'

What was the secret of her eternal youth? Simply to face the passage of time: neither the past nor the future with its mysteries abashed her. In 1699 Saint-Evremond wrote to her: 'You are of all countries and all time . . . mistress of the present as of the past!' And Ninon replied: 'There are few who can make head against the years; but I think I have not yet let them overwhelm me.' In fact she never went into mourning for her vanished youth, or the passing of her beauty. 'Wrinkles are the mark of wisdom,' she wrote to Saint-Evremond. There was a bold pronouncement for a woman! And as aforetime, Ninon growing old, Ninon in old age, was still haloed with her charm: still she was able to fascinate society by the originality of all that she said, and by the delicacy in which she wrapped her very scepticism.

Did she keep to her freethinking ways to the end of her life? Certain it is that she had Christian burial—she may even have received extreme unction. In the last months of her life, the Church tried to save her soul. Then it was that she said to Fontenelle: 'You know the profit I might have made of my body; and I could still make a better bargain for my soul, for the Jesuits and the Jansenists are bidding for it.'

A little before her death, the Abbé de Châteauneuf brought her his protégé, François-Marie Arouet, then eleven years old. The boy was hardly able to conceal his emotion, so frightened was he by the parchment complexion of the aged Ninon. But she was charmed by the liveliness of his wit, and urged him to cultivate poetry, as Voltaire (who was that boy) later wrote to a friend. Besides, she left him a legacy of one thousand francs 'to buy books'.

In the course of her long life Ninon saw the birth of a society that was soon to take the path towards a troubled uncertain destiny, but it was still bathed in the light of the Great Century, that firmly hewn, robust, imposing era. In the dawn on the new age Ninon showed the way to what was to be the essence of the eighteenth century; the supremacy of intellect over virtue, and the questioning of all traditional values.

CHAPTER FOUR

FREE THOUGHT AND PHILOSOPHY

DELIGHTS OF SOCIETY

'The delights of society and of conversation are pleasures equal to the charm of a rendez-vous during one's youth,' wrote Voltaire to Madame du Deffand.

In fact society was never more brilliant or conversation more sparkling than in that century of light, the eighteenth. The vitality of this talk throbs even in the letters, conveying to the reader the tingling champagne bubble of the dialogue. It echoes melodiously in the letters which Madame du Deffand sends to Walpole in England, it electrifies the letters of Voltaire, exiled at the Court of the King of Prussia.

In the *salons*, the finishing-school of gracious living, the 'regulars' learn how to express themselves with delicacy and refinement. With the latter, the interior of the house is in tune: silken boudoirs, cosy drawing-rooms, luxurious armchairs and sofas, graceful *consoles* and *bonheurs-du-jour*—a wealth of well-being, the ideal setting for a light conversation, seasoned with savoury anecdotes. But who would suspect that in these apparently frivolous surroundings a complete overthrow of principles is being planned and the weapons of a future rebellion forged?

The very fashions seem to have been expressly devised to add a note of levity to the feminine image. Countless paintings and engravings show us smart and seductive ladies, attended by fashionable abbés and the inevitable *cicisbeo*. Naturally, these ladies have a gallant; educated in convents, married very young, almost in childhood, to husbands older by far than themselves, how could they live without love? But in the confessional many faults are forgiven, for the confessor too is a man of his time.

It is a frivolous age, yes, and there is abundant evidence for this. Yet there is another eighteenth century, if we will look further into it. And the more we explore, the greater the depths we find. In them we see a very different picture of woman from the accepted stereotype. She may be neither wife nor mother, having exchanged the sanctity of marriage for a new morality.

For an example of the misunderstood and undervalued Frenchwoman of the eighteenth century we need look no further than the Marquise de Pompadour. And very typical she is. Generations of the ignorant have seen in her only an adventuress rising quickly to dizzy heights, mistress of the royal harem, fit heroine for a novelette. But the study of her letters, of which hundreds are extant, brings to light quite another Pompadour. In a fine and graceful hand she gives minutely elaborate instructions to architects and painters, and with wholly masculine efficiency she organizes the founding of the *École Militaire*. Her protection of the philosophers did not stop at obtaining the royal favour. She knew the worth of the Encyclopaedists, defended Montesquieu against his detractors, and bid defiance to the hate of the clerical party by commanding a performance of *Tartuffe* at the Petite Galerie in the royal apartments.

Those who wished to be virtuous did not rely on religious dogma but on their own free will. And to be virtuous, in that century of light, meant to fight againt obscurantism, to prefer the visible to the probable, the self-evident to the uncertain. Of course the human spirit is subject to passions, but to fight them would involve psychological dangers. It is civil law, not canon law, that can keep the passions in check, and only reason can moderate them.

A few chosen spirits meet at the houses of great ladies, on which they confer international repute; those of Madame de Lambert, Madame du Deffand, Madame Geoffrin . . . here scientific problems are discussed, here the spirit of toleration is cultivated and the new philosophy takes shape.

Gone are the poets with their occasional verses dedicated to ladies, gone are the pampered authors of the previous century. In this new climate it is impossible to imagine anything so vapid as the *Garland for Julie* or the *Chart of Emotions*!

Conversation tackles major problems: interest in progress and in scientific research grows and grows. There is a wealth of efforts to enlighten and awaken the conscience of the public.

Curiosity does not stop at frontiers. Whereas the men of the seventeenth century stayed at home, those of the next travel. The goal of their journeys was not, as in modern times, the enjoyment of foreign scenery and works of art, but simply to establish contact with foreign intellectuals. Truly cosompolitan, they felt at home in educated circles throughout Europe. The true cosmopolitan put this cultivated Europe above his country, in the same way as he put his country above his family.

The despotism of the Sun King had throttled freedom of expression. Intolerance, the fruit of schemings by Madame de Maintenon and the clergy, had borne hard on the intellectuals, and the idea of royal omnipotence continued to cloud their consciousness.

But now a new breeze is blowing through the minds of men, a breeze of rebellion and liberty. The boldness of English writers, critical of law, of government, of the King himself, arouses enthusiasm. 'How I love the bold English!' Voltaire exclaims. 'How I love people who say what they think!'

In France, too, and notably in the *salons*, people begin to say what they think. Thought and speech and writing run together. People write as they speak, without verbal decoration or metaphor. The language, once more purged—this time of preciosity—crystallizes until it is as clear as the thought which it conveys.

Compared with the complacently sophisticated dialect of modern scientific writing, that of the eighteenth century shows a maximum of clarity. No writer then would have dreamed of composing high-flown lectures, suggesting to the reader that he too is numbered among the superior beings. Self-expression, in speech as in writing, if couched in pretentious terms, counted as want of politeness, especially towards ladies.

If the subject of conversation had changed, so also had the audience of the *salons*. Now they consist of doctors, chemists, scientific researchers—'natural philosophers' as they were still called in England. But all are philosophers in some sense, or claim to be. Even Marivaux, the lightest of literary minds, calls himself a philosopher, for he too wants to upset the idols of past time and set up a new morality.

Discussion, free of all restraint, allows itself free rein. 'Let everyone find happiness as he understands it,' Frederick II's motto, served as the password in 'philosophical' circles. 'As he understands it' might mean for some, organizing opposition to the King, the Court and the clergy; to others, making education accessible to the greatest possible number of people, arming them with the spiritual weapon of the middle class.

On the surface then, this is an Arcadia, a perpetual barqueload bound for Cythera. But below the surface there is doubt and mistrust, anxiety, melancholia; all the makings of a day when the laughter will die on their lips.

SMART PARTIES AND SOMBRE SPEECH

After the Sun King was dead, and bigotry with him, the Court was once more full of the joy of life. The Regent, Philippe d'Orléans, the very model of a rake, debauched and given over to pleasure, gave licence full rein and established a new style for high society. His Regency (1715–23) was one long entertainment, a never-ending smart party.

Likewise at Sceaux, where the Duchesse du Maine kept state, with her wit and imagination, pleasure succeeded pleasure, with ballets and plays and masked balls. Watteau's pictures seem to live again in the sparkling evenings of Sceaux.

The world of the Regency, with its florid poetic elegance, had much to attract slightly decadent late nineteenth-century authors such as the Goncourt brothers (Wilde would have been at home there, and Aubrey Beardsley delighted in drawing characters in the costume of the period). Such retrospective admirers were attracted by personalities such as the Duchesse du Maine, or the Comtesse de Boufflers, who was the Prince de Conti's mistress. What corresponded in English terms to the early Georgian peerage made good copy for such novelists. And no doubt they were adept at reconstructing the delicately perfumed atmosphere of these *salons*, but they could not look into the depths of the wave that swept away men's minds towards a new world.

For some years the attractions of the Regency bid fair to eclipse the *salons* altogether. But already, from one circle at least, gaming and gossip are banned, and there the pomp and luxury of the Court are severely criticized. Thus at Madame de Lambert's, a veritable office of wit, resorted to by those in flight from the noise and bustle of the world, celebrities like Montesquieu and Fontenelle congregate.

Doubtless Madame de Lambert was a little out of the fashion, an added attraction at a time when the fashionable world strove so hard to be up to date. Perhaps she herself even hankered for the times of the Hôtel de Rambouillet, where, as she was so fond of saying 'the Graces and the Muses agreed so well together'.

She was dedicated to morality. Is that because she was the daughter of a lady of dubious reputation? Be that as it may, in her house consciences are scrupulously examined, tradition is respected, humanitarianism is the order of the day. But that is not to say that Madame de Lambert, who bubbled with vitality, had any leanings towards bigotry or pedantry.

She was only a moralist in the highest, that is, the philosophic sense. She seems to be among the forerunners of the revolution when she exclaims: 'Those who think commonly and basely I call vulgar. And the Court is full of them.'

Everything that passes through her mind, everything that she learns in the course of conversation, everything that she wishes to impart to her children, she notes down. But against her wishes her *Advice to a Son* and *Reflections on Women* are incorporated in an anthology and published. Outraged, she tries to buy up the whole edition, but too late, for many copies have already been sold to the public.

The writings of Madame de Lambert are the best guide to the way people thought in those first three decades of the century. They are such an amusing mixture of propriety and free thought. And such penetrating feminine psychology. Here are a few of her reflections:

'We educate women for love, but in the process we forbid them to practise it—It is very hard for a woman to be virtuous, for there is no fame attached to virtue—The most lively passions need modesty in order to show themselves in an attractive form.' And then again, the height of feminine subtlety: 'Modesty is so essential to pleasure that one must retain it even at those times when one is trying to dispense with it.'

She proclaims that women must educate themselves, must be cultivated. But Molière, with *Les Femmes savantes*, did them a great disservice. 'Ever since then,' she writes, 'as much disgrace has been attached to feminine learning as to the most strictly forbidden vices.' Shame for shame 'Women choose the easiest: pleasure.'

Although many mocked at her little books, people fought to read them, and the few copies in circulation fetched their weight in gold. For women they represented a manual of the customs of high society and showed them how to keep conversation alive. More than that, they contain advice that is still valid today. 'Making fun of people, which is one of the amusements of conversation, is hard to manage . . . for it's but a step from the gentlest fun to that which will cause offence . . . and it should only be aimed at the very slightest faults, so that the butt of it jokes about them himself.'

Madame de Lambert's *salon* became the antechamber of the Academy, which was going through a period of stagnation. But once her protégés were admitted, such as Fontenelle, Lamotte and above all Montesquieu, that institution was transformed. Montesquieu would never have been elected, after his ironic observations about the Academy in the *Lettres persanes*, had it not been for the intervention of Madame de Lambert. So the new philosophy entered at last into that hieratic and solemn institution.

The reputation of the Parisian *salons* spread far beyond the frontiers, until foreign visitors of distinction no longer sought letters of recommendation to the Court but to certain great ladies without whose favour they could not succeed, either in society or in some diplomatic mission.

More than one political reputation was made or marred, for foreigners, in the *salon* of Madame de Tencin. Without a word from her to the Regent—she had been one of his many mistresses—the famous Scottish financier John Law would never have been able to put his adventurous enterprises into execution. But Madame de Tencin was not able to foresee the disastrous results of Law's financial system, the introduction of paper money and the catastrophic bankruptcies that came in its train.

On the other hand, she had a sure instinct for intellectual values and for new and revolutionary ideas. Thus, right from the publication of *L'Esprit de Lois* she realized its importance, and bought most of the first impression to distribute among her friends.

Her rise to social heights is reminiscent of Ninon's. For Madame de Tencin too had the same sort of professional career behind her. Yet she had been convent-educated; she had even taken vows. But the convent in question was that of the Dames Augustines near Grenoble, well-known for its worldliness, and in its parlours many a promising love affair had taken shape.

The Marshal de Richelieu, a contemporary, wrote: 'Her

graces, her wit, and her very free conversation had drawn to the convent all the licentious spirits of Grenoble, whether civil or military.'

The reputation of the beautiful and lightly-loving Alexandrine de Tencin made short work of scaling the convent walls. Until the day when she herself went over the wall, and in her flight made for the spot best calculated to satisfy her ambitions: Paris.

There she embarked on a dissolute life. The suicide of one of her numerous lovers in her house was an annoying circumstance that cost her three months in the Bastille, but only one of many such, in her adventurous life. Her talent for intrigue is proved by her very mediocre brother's appointment to the see of Lyon, owing his archbishopric to her. But perhaps she regretted later having left her new-born baby which she had by the Chevalier Destouches as a foundling in a church porch—this was one fine day in November 1717—for the boy, brought up by the wife of a glazier, grew up to be the celebrated mathematician and philosopher d'Alembert.

Madame de Tencin aimed high; at entry into the great world. Her rapid rise into high society was equalled only by the celerity with which she changed from an adventuress into a genuine great lady. During the last ten years of her life Fontenelle, Mairan, Marivaux, Montesquieu and Helvétius were some of the great minds who were regularly to be found in the drawing-room.

MADAME GEOFFRIN

Chardin, the painter of middle-class conversation pieces, was the only fit artist to transmit to posterity the authentic likeness of Madame Geoffrin: look at his portrait of her, seated in an arm-chair, in a dress that seems a little out of fashion, in her lace cap, with her rather heavy features. No, she is not the model for a painter of airy nymphs, or of fashionable women.

Indeed, Madame Geoffrin is anything but smart. Middle-class by birth, orphaned in youth, she was brought up by her grand-mother along old-fashioned lines. What do young girls want with education, asked her grandmother; all she needs is to preserve the gifts God gave her. She might learn to read, certainly, but write . . .? What would be the good of that? And so Madame Geoffrin, even when well on in years, still astonished her friends by the eccentricities of her spelling.

At sixteen she was married to the respected Monsieur Geoffrin, her elder by thirty-four years; a man who had started from nothing and made a tidy fortune, becoming Inspector of Taxes for Saint-Gobain.

Her household breathed middle-class respectability. Her life was almost cloistered; she rose at dawn, never went to dances or dinners, and only very rarely to the theatre. Was she beautiful as a young woman? We do not know; certainly she was not gay and never went near a fashionable milliner's.

And most certainly she never had a gallant. Baron Gleichen, Danish Ambassador at Paris, wrote: 'She was very virtuous, though her husband was ugly and stupid.' Monsieur Geoffrin, according to Gleichen, had only one hobby: playing the *trompette marine*—a single-stringed instrument. He tried to educate himself by reading an encyclopaedia which was printed in double column, but as he insisted on reading straight across the page, he gave it up, declaring in despair that he could not understand what it was all about.

The first years of their married life passed uneventfully. But—and this was to be decisive for the future—there lived in the same street, the Rue St-Honoré, the beautiful and witty Madame de Tencin. Between these two women, otherwise so unlike, a solid friendship was formed. And then one day—it was in 1730—Madame Geoffrin made her bow in the Tencin *salon*, meeting there people much to her taste, and much superior to those she had known hitherto. Now, since she had a big house with elegantly furnished rooms, she got ready to invite all the regular guests of Madame de Tencin.

This worried her husband, who flew into a rage; he saw no point in spending his good money on anything so frivolous as a supper. An altercation followed. All was in vain; at last he arrived at the only possible compromise: silence.

Monsieur Geoffrin died in 1740 at the age of eighty-four. Not long after his death, one of her friends asked Madame Geoffrin: 'What became of the silent old gentleman who always sat at the foot of the table?' Madame Geoffrin: 'That was my husband: he died.'

Madame Geoffrin had one daughter, Madame de la Ferté—'the cuckoo's egg I hatched'. She lived in the same house, perpetually at odds with her mother. Did she, like so many young people, hold advanced views? Not at all: she was a reactionary, hating the new seditious philosophy and finding no good word for the Encyclopaedists, those destroyers of morality. She too held a *salon*, frequented by the smart set, where she made mock of her mother's friends. They were railed at, mimicked, and their works parodied. The fame of Madame de la Ferté crossed the frontiers when she created the Order of Lanturlus, a mock academy, which in the end a number of members of note, both French and foreign, flocked to join.

Madame de Tencin died in 1749 and Madame Geoffrin fell sole heir to her *salon*; but much more than her predecessor, she understood how to attract the great writers and philosophers: Diderot, d'Alembert, Marmontel, Helvétius, Holbach, Grimm, as well as the now aged Fontenelle, who had known Madame de Sévigné and Madame de La Fayette.

Despite her apparent and unconcealed simplicity, Madame Geoffrin was not lacking in snobbery: none but the most celebrated personalities will do for her, and the most conspicuous ones at that. Conspicuous but not outrageous: for always she is on the quest for good taste and impeccable manners, Voltaire with his acid talk seems to have irritated her; later, she even refused to subscribe to the statue which it was proposed to put up to him.

She maintained the same withdrawn attitude towards Diderot, whose character contained all elements calculated to shock her: excessively temperamental, with a mixture of personal coarseness and subtlety. Instinctively, she felt that the exuberant fantasy of this great man passed over her head. But her note on this is not without observation: 'Diderot is always like a man dreaming, and believing in all that he dreams.'

Madame Geoffrin was at once shrewd and limited, petty and generous. When in 1759 the privileges granted to the *Grande Encyclopédie* were revoked by royal edict, she advanced a hundred thousand crowns to the publisher, asking besides to remain anonymous. Without her generosity, Diderot, who was heavily in debt, would not have been able to escape total ruin.

It is not easy to form a clear picture of Madame Geoffrin. Sometimes she seems middle-class and pedantic, solemn and moralizing, and at other times like a great lady of quality, with a personality compelling enough to have drawn many leading personalities into her orbit. Contemporary opinions of her likewise are conflicting, the aristocrats finding her too homely and the wits too didactic. Thus Baron Gleichen, who knew her at the height of her fame: 'Her plain speech and her middle-class tone gave her conversation, which was full of wisdom and sense, a piquant and sometimes a sublime quality.'

When receiving guests she liked to sound motherly and didactic. She would say again and again, 'That's good' or 'Let us be agreeable', according to Marmontel. On the other hand, no one knew better than she how to amuse the company with humorous comment and saucy repartee. Still in old age she could amuse the young: 'I make them faint with laughter.' Even d'Alembert, in the early days of Madame Geoffrin's *salon*, appeared brimming with gaiety 'like a schoolboy playing truant' in the words of a contemporary. In fact, nothing gave grounds for foreseeing his melancholy end.

Reading their own works to Madame Geoffrin became a real hobby for writers, who found her comments extraordinarily acute. Her delightful conversation, her sallies, which were bandied around Paris just as the stupid remarks of her late husband had been, all contributed to make her *salon* one of the most celebrated in all Paris.

Madame Geoffrin made an innovation. She replaced the traditional supper by a dinner—at the hour when we take luncheon nowadays—and kept up the habit to the end. Happy were those days when there was time and to spare; conversation went on until late in the afternoon.

There is one point on which her contemporaries agree without dispute: all gastronomic pleasure was utterly absent from those dinners. Invariably the menu consisted of chicken, spinach, and omelettes; or else of omelettes, chicken, and spinach.

It is all to the honour of Madame Geoffrin to have invited artists also, for at the time this meant a liberal, even a democratic spirit. Later, she was to add art connoisseurs and archaeologists. But she insisted on drawing one distinction: the literary and philosophic dinners took place on Wednesdays, whereas on Mondays artists and architects dined with her, such as Greuze, Lemoyne, Soufflot, Vernet, Cochin, La Tour, Boucher, Vanloo. Often too she went to see them in their studios and bought their pictures, which eventually filled her house. Anyone in our day who wants to know what pictures fetched then can look up the prices in her meticulously kept accounts, which form some reading of interest.

Marmontel, forgotten nowadays—unjustly so, for his article on Toleration in the *Grande Encyclopédie* is a magnanimous masterpiece—has preserved in his memoirs more than one amusing anecdote of those dinners for painters. 'I had no difficulty in noticing,' he writes, 'that though they had natural wit they lacked all education and polish—or most of them did.' His pen does not even spare Soufflot, whose narrowness of outlook he deplores. 'His thought was confined within the limits drawn by his compass.' And Boucher 'painted Venus and the Virgin like chorus girls; and his language, like his pictures, put one in mind of his models'. On the other hand, La Tour painted portraits of philosophers but was 'embarrassed when one talked to him about painting'.

Madame Geoffrin's ambitions grew with success. She aimed to make her *salon* an international gathering, bringing together eminent personalities of all countries. This she achieved, and her success was to have reverberations that went far beyond her original intent. By establishing contact between the great men of France and foreigners, she contributed largely to the diffusion of French culture abroad.

Who can call the entire roll of foreign celebrities who rubbed elbows in her house: Baron Gleichen, David Hume, leader of the British school of sceptical empiricists, Gibbon, the historian, Caraccioli, the Neapolitan diplomat and freethinker, the witty Abbé Galiani, that 'harlequin with the brains of a Macchiavelli', Baron Melchior Grimm, an acute observer and caustic chronicler; and many, many others.

Benjamin Franklin also visited her in 1767; but as she wrote to Hume: 'Of M. Franklin, who does not speak French, I only saw the reputation.'

The familiar tone of her speech is recognizable in her letters. Writing to David Hume, she calls him 'rogue' or 'my great joker'. She mocks him because he sends her his works in luxurious bindings while his private library seems clad in paupers' rags.

Hume had commended Horace Walpole to her. This son of the great English statesman was at first enchanted with the intuitive good sense, the lucid judgment of Madame Geoffrin.

But his enthusiasm was short-lived. He soon deserted to the rival *salon* kept by Madame du Deffand.

The one weakness of Madame Geoffrin was her idolization of crowned heads. She managed to entertain Gustavus III of Sweden and Joseph II of Austria. But who could foresee the destiny of the young Pole who called her *Maman* and whom she saved from prison by paying his debts? This rake is none other than Stanislas Poniatowski, launched by Madame Geoffrin into Parisian society. Thence he left for St Petersburg, to become the lover of Catherine the Great, who was then only a Grand Duchess; to her he owed the favour and the intrigues which led to his becoming crowned King of Poland. Later the Empress was to write to Madame Geoffrin: 'How he became king I really do not know; only because Providence willed it so.'

In 1764, no sooner was he crowned than Stanislas wrote to Madame Geoffrin: 'Dear *Maman*, my reign has begun, do not scold me.'

Madame Geoffrin is carried away with joy and enthusiasm. She must set off at once to see at close quarters the kingdom of her 'adopted son' as she calls him. But two years are to pass before the dream is fulfilled. At last, in 1766, she left Paris, in comfort, driving in a large Berlin, and accompanied only by several servants. Immersed in her meditations, she did not even look out of the window. Landscape never moved her, only people.

The journey to Vienna took three weeks. Prince Kaunitz, Chancellor to the Empress, had carefully prepared everything for her arrival. Later, on her return to Paris, she was to send him her portrait which, as she wrote, 'only shows the dull features of an old woman'. The Chancellor sent her his, but on such a large canvas that it could not be got through the door of her *salon*, so that a miniature had to be copied from it. At Vienna Prince Galitzin asked her to stay in his palace, but Madame Geoffrin preferred to stop at an inn, where the Prince sent her coffee with milk every morning.

The Empress Maria Theresa received her at Schönbrunn, and she was introduced to the whole Court; she also saw Marie-Antoinette, then eleven years old. 'The Emperor's daughter is here,' Madame Geoffrin wrote to a friend in Paris, 'as pretty as an angel. The Empress asks me to make this known in Paris.'

A courier from the King of Poland came to fetch Madame

Geoffrin from Vienna. He had orders to arrange her journey in all possible comfort, as a queen might travel; he therefore brought with him a wagon full of furniture, tableware, silver and provisions, to be used at every inn where the traveller would stay.

At last she was in Poland, at Warsaw. But what a disappointment! She was appalled by the untidiness, the muddle, the dirt of the country, the prejudices of the people, the religious intolerance. She formed the impression of a medieval empire. She had some stormy interviews with the King, flatly telling him her opinion of his country. A chapter of her life was closed. All that remained was to forget this disappointment. Only Walpole, in spiteful mockery, was in future to call her nothing but Geoffrinska, in mock-Polish.

In Paris, Grimm marvelled: how could a woman of sixty-eight who had never in her life been farther than the suburbs of Paris, possibly undertake such a journey? 'What first appeared ridiculous and even foolhardy,' he wrote, 'suddenly seems fine and interesting.'

Now Madame Geoffrin could add one more specimen to her collection of majesties. In 1762 the Grand Duchess Catherine, with whom she had been corresponding for the past ten years, was proclaimed Empress of Russia. The pen friendship between the middle-class Parisienne and the Tsarina was to last another fifteen years, and there is no doubt that Madame Geoffrin intended to visit Russia, for the Empress asked her not to stand on ceremony and treat her 'like the Grand Sophy of Persia—there's nothing uglier than greatness', she added.

Madame Geoffrin never could refrain from moralizing, even in her letters to Catherine the Great. When the Tsarina, after her husband Peter III had been assassinated, issued a ukase giving out that it was an accident, Madame Geoffrin seems to have expressed her scruples to her, for the Empress raged: 'This edict was not drawn up for the benefit of foreign countries, it was composed for a people who have to be told what they ought to believe.'

For all that, there was a witness who knew exactly what had taken place. Rulhière, secretary to the Embassy at St Petersburg wrote his *Anecdotes of the Revolution in Russia in 1762* as soon as he got back to Paris in that same year. In it he set down in black and white how Peter III, in spite of having renounced the throne, was assassinated on the orders of Alexei Orloff, lover of Catherine the Great.

This was read in manuscript at Madame Geoffrin's, in the presence of Grimm, Baron Gleichen, of a prince related to the King of Poland, and of other persons. Echo of it came to the ears of the Empress. She set everything in motion, either to gain possession of the manuscript or to destroy it. To this end, Madame Geoffrin offered the author fabulous sums, but in vain. However, the *Anecdotes* were not published until 1797, after the Empress was dead.

Catherine the Great's admiration for the progress of science and philosophy in France is notorious. In more than one of her letters to Madame Geoffrin she gives vent to this enthusiasm, especially for Montesquieu: 'His *Esprit des Lois* is a handbook for monarchs, if only they had the common sense to realize it,' and she adds: 'Were I the Pope, I should canonize him.'

Unfortunately Madame Geoffrin's letters have been lost. But those that Catherine the Great wrote to her, lively and humorous masterpieces, delightfully unrestrained, reveal a whole chapter of her private life. Her reflexions about her empire are just like the remarks of a householder about her establishment. When she describes herself in almost elementary style, running over the articles of the constitution every morning, she seems to be concerned with kitchen recipes. And the untidiness of her private quarters! Tables tottering under the weight of books. 'The ladies of Paris would faint,' she writes in 1765, 'to see the stormy life I lead.'

The winter of 1766 brought this letter from her country house to Madame Geoffrin: 'You ask what I am doing? I read, I write, I go for drives in my sleigh, I shoot woodcock, I gamble; I live.'

It seems that Madame Geoffrin must have complimented her on this energetic life, and that Prince Orloff read the letter, for the Tsarina writes: 'He who makes a profession of laziness exclaimed: "How true!"' These were the days of her love for the man who had taken the place in her heart once occupied by Stanislas Poniatowski—indeed, for her this was living!

The Empress had generously rescued Diderot from his financial shipwreck, as once Madame Geoffrin had done. She asked him to the Winter Palace at St Petersburg in 1773, being perhaps less shocked than the ladies of Paris by his familiar manner. In her letters to Madame Geoffrin she only complains that in the ardour of his conversation Diderot cannot refrain from gesticulating: 'After every conversation with him my thighs are black with bruises. I had to put a table between him and myself.'

Only very rarely does Madame Geoffrin entertain ladies who, in her words, 'slide the conversation from the profound to the superficial'. But she does make an exception in favour of Madame Necker. Would she have invited her so often if she had been able to foresee the unfavourable remarks that were to be published some years later by that prim Swiss in her memoirs?

But one of Madame Necker's remarks is very penetrating: 'Old age for some is the limit of their life: but Madame Geoffrin has made it the goal of hers.'

Of course Madame Geoffrin fancied herself in the part of The Old Lady: she took full advantage of all the honours which are due to seniority, but towards the end of her life the intellectual freedom which had prevailed in her circle was no more. She even found herself hoping that the philosophers would give up free-thinking as regards religion; she would have liked them to take the sacrament regularly and turn their thoughts on felicity in the hereafter. She affected not to understand politics, and asked all her guests to refrain from expressing any sort of political conviction that might be construed as subversive. Says Grimm, ironically: 'Mother Geoffrin, in whose house one may talk neither of court matters, nor town matters, nor affairs of East or West, nor politics, nor finance, nor religion, nor government, nor theology, nor metaphysics. . . .'

She died in 1777 aged seventy-eight. Turgot wrote: 'She had not really been alive for the past year.'

MADAME DU DEFFAND

Madame du Deffand was Madame Geoffrin's contemporary, and the same company rubbed shoulders in their *salons*. Yet neither Madame Geoffrin nor other feminine celebrities of the day could compare with Madame du Deffand. In reading her letters we cannot miss the beams of her sharp intelligence, her clear intuition, and even today her wit exalts and galvanizes us. Poor Madame Geoffrin! Eclipsed by such an exceptional rival, how can she appear otherwise than as a virtuous and moralizing lady, encouraging artists and protecting philosophers. We are in danger of forgetting that in her house the seeds of the greatest ideas of her time sprouted.

As for Madame du Deffand, she encouraged neither artists nor philosophers. She bid defiance to her times and to men, according to her mood. Now gay, now pensive, she is by turns devout and atheistic, avid of company and profoundly solitary. Her admiration both for things and people has its limits, and finally she turns on herself in derision, going so far as to say: 'What I hate most and would gladly flee from, is myself.'

Marie de Vichy-Chamrond, born in 1697, came from Burgundy, as did Madame de Sévigné and Colette. She went to school at one of those convents which were hatching-grounds for the smart set, and marriage for her, as for so many young women of her background, signified only escape.

It did not take her long to find out how monotonous life with her husband, the Marquis du Deffand, could be. His young wife was bored. But she was pretty, charming, sprightly, she went everywhere—to the Luxembourg, to the Duchesse de Berry's parties, to the Palais-Royal, to Saint-Cloud, to the Regent's entertainments (indeed she was his mistress for some weeks: fleeting as the liaison was, it paid her well, since it was rewarded with a life annuity of six thousand ducats).

Once the Regent was dead and the taste of the times had turned away from frivolity and profligacy, she made an attempt to resume conjugal relations with her husband, first at their country place and then at Paris. But the temptations of the capital were irresistible, and the young Marquise did not resist them. She packed her dull husband off to their country house.

She would have had to lead a very dissolute life indeed to arouse scandal among Parisian society, which was tolerant in matters of love. As it was, she was as welcome as anyone at Sceaux, the Duchesse du Maine's country house. Here the entertainments were less brassy and spectacular than they were at Saint-Cloud. The glittering wit of Madame du Deffand, her beauty, her clarity of judgment, the charm of her intelligence, all caused a sensation. She formed a lasting attachment to the Duchesse du Maine, the kind of loving friendship that united Madame Récamier and Madame de Staël. The correspondence between Madame du Deffand and the Duchesse is warmed by the same sort of the tender affection.

Among the friends of the Duchesse, Madame du Deffand met and was attracted to Madame de Staal Delaunay, who like her was keenly interested in people and like her took love lightly (and often). It having become known that Madame de Staal had written her memoirs, one of her friends asked her, 'How have you dealt with your love life?' to which she replied 'Oh well, it's only a portrait from the waist upwards.'

In these memoirs she draws the portrait of Madame du Deffand according to the fashion of the times: 'The sparkling fire that enlivens her gets to the very bottom of every subject, brings it out of itself and brings all its features into relief. Hers in supreme degree is the talent for painting characters, and her portraits are more alive than the originals, giving us a better idea of their nature than the most intimate acquaintance would do.'

She met young Voltaire again at Sceaux, having first made his acquaintance at the Regent's Court. At that time he was trying his hand at poetry; but by now his literary star was in the ascendant.

Also at Sceaux her relationship with President Hénault began. He was a playwright of only middling competence, a widower for some time past, in advanced middle age, who had been elected to the Academy on the strength of his historical works, which were to the taste of the members. Their union was not a passionate one but was based on mutual esteem. It bore much resemblance to a *mariage de raison*, and was to last till the death of the President in 1770. In the end his company, his smart connections, his advice, became indispensable to the Marquise. In old age she wrote: 'As for my rouge, as for the President, never shall I do them the honour of deserting them.'

About 1740 Madame du Deffand began to receive in her house in the Rue de Beaune, the same house where Voltaire passed the last days of his life. Her activity is tireless. In her *salon*, visiting friends, always and everywhere, she shines, she fascinates, she enlivens the conversation by her lively and enjoyable quips, such as the one about supper: 'it is one of the four aims of man: I have forgotten the other three.'

Those suppers at Madame du Deffand's! Round a table spread with the most exquisite dishes and the finest wines veritable philosophic jousts take place between her and the celebrities of the period, where bold and novel theses are freely exchanged and all preciosity is banished. Madame du Deffand said herself: 'These little gatherings are the very antithesis of the late Hôtel de Rambouillet.' Montesquieu on his travels looked back with longing to those unforgettable evenings: 'Nothing I can get to read can fill the place of a quarter of an hour at those delectable supper parties.'

But the real miracle, which will have far-reaching consequences, is that Madame du Deffand allowed the *esprit frondeur*, that irreverent, aggressive, questioning essence of the century, to rule in her *salon*. All respect for rank and station are out of place here, where the higher nobility meets the foremost thinkers, with men of science, with artists; and, as a class, is preparing its own downfall.

At these meetings revolutionary theories of the theatrical revolution to come are discussed. Not content with listening to professional stars like Lekain and Clairon, who, also as guests of the Marquise, give excerpts from famous works, the audience comes to life and proclaims such doctrines as: the theatre must not be an idealization, it must show life as it is; from now on it must struggle against injustice and for tolerance. Of course it is not yet as much as a plea for a *committed* theatre; but the new tendencies will be manifest, as Voltaire says, 'in a pure morality which is innate in the subject yet does not show itself'.

In 1747 Madame du Deffand left her house in the Rue de Beaune to take up residence in the Convent St Joseph, in the elegant little set of chambers where Madame de Montespan had once lived. There she could discharge her religious obligations; a door led from her bedroom direct to the chapel, where she had a permanent pew, rented rather like a box in the theatre.

Her manner of life was as capricious as the mind it reflected. Her true life began only at night, by candlelight, and her sight began to fail. Soon she only saw things as through a veil, outlines getting more and more blurred. In 1752 she laments in a letter to Montesquieu her approaching blindness, and he tries to console her: 'Those who can see are none the better illuminated for all that.' A year after that, she was wholly blind, and Voltaire said to a friend: 'At least Madame du Deffand still has her wits, which were of more quality than her eyes.'

Surrounded by faithful and devoted friends, Madame du Deffand spares no one with her caustic tongue. She has no faith in the sincerity of her contemporaries in search of an ideal, or in their efforts to convert her; she deflates their exaltation. Her perpetual need to tear apart the veil of social convention and get down to the naked personality, observing all its weaknesses and mistakes, drives her to cynicism and often to calumny. She loathes Rousseau and doubts his sincerity: she does not like his works, considers his *Social Contract* boring and obscure and his *Héloïse* contrary to common sense.

Rousseau did not fail to take revenge. He says in his *Confessions* that communication between himself and Madame du Deffand was impossible, if only because she went to bed about the time he got up. He notes her 'despotism, and the oracular fits', her 'incredible prejudices', her 'passion for second-rate intellects, the importance that she attached, for good or ill, to minute trifles . . . I took less notice of her, and she perceived it.' When the *Confessions* came out, Madame du Deffand wrote to Voltaire: 'I would rather expose myself to the scourge of his enmity than to that of his friendship.'

INTERMEZZO: THE RIVAL

Just about the time when she was losing her sight Madame du Deffand took a lively interest in Julie de Lespinasse, natural daughter of her brother, Comte Gaspard de Vichy. Since childhood Julie had suffered the pitiless inhumanity of an aristocracy that not only ignored but actually humiliated the illegitimate child; once her mother, the Comtesse d'Albon, was dead she had been deprived of the large fortune to which she was entitled. Between her and Madame du Deffand a correspondence began.

It would be difficult to imagine more affectionate and more maternal letters than those from Madame du Deffand to this young girl. She calls her 'my queen' and says that if she came to keep her company she would introduce her to a world of spiritual riches and would treat her as a member of her own family, glossing over her origins with the greatest discretion. But also she warns her: 'The slightest artifice, the least airs and graces that you put on with me, would not be borne with. I am naturally mistrustful, and all those in whom I think I see too much subtlety are suspect to the point where I can no longer trust them . . . so you must be resolved to live with me in the utmost truth and sincerity.'

So Julie came. She was twenty, intelligent, avid for instruction, of a pleasant appearance. Did Madame du Deffand exploit her? Members of the philosophical set have gone so far as to assert this, and still today certain biographers of Julie de Lespinasse have taken up their stance. Certain it is that Madame du Deffand's nature was a complex one, and that she was difficult to live with. Julie, obliged to fall in with her extravagant habits, had to turn night into day and day into night, as she did. The core of her new occupation was to choose books, to seek out the most interesting passages, and to read them to Madame du Deffand. This cannot have been a dull task—rather, an agreeable one! The time was coming when Julie would be able to impress the intellectuals by this knowledge which she had so abundantly accumulated.

At the parties and suppers which the Marquise gives, Julie becomes the centre of attraction. She is admired, adored, flattered. Old President Hénault dances attendance on her, waxes lyrical, constantly compliments her on her appearance, on her brilliant wit. Carmontelle paints her portrait, Turgot takes a keen interest in her; and above all, and more than all, d'Alembert.

Soon she was to become known as the 'Regentess'. And Madame du Deffand, with the acute hearing of the blind, began to guess. She guessed how many visitors Julie was receiving in her suite at the Convent St Joseph, and sensed the growing importance of her rival. Suspicion became certainty, and Madame du Deffand refused any longer to nourish a viper in her bosom. After ten years of cohabitation, she provoked a break in their relationship.

Julie de Lespinasse rented a small suite in the Rue de Bellechasse, only a few steps from the convent. Her friends helped her to move in, and 'made interest' with the King to procure her a life annuity. Visitors flocked to her between the Geoffrin dinners and the Deffand suppers. One and all they came, the flower of literature and science: d'Alembert, Turgot, Condillac, Marmontel, Malesherbes, Diderot, the young Condorcet, Laharpe, Bernardin de Saint-Pierre, Grimm, Baron Gleichen. Grimm writes that every day he found not less than thirty to forty visitors in the suite.

Whence this immense success? All felt themselves at their ease. In contrast to Madame du Deffand, where lesser intellects were sniped at and the great grumbled against, perfect harmony reigned at Julie's. Her *forte* was in reconciling her guests to the most hostile ideologies. 'When they were there,' writes Marmontel, 'they were like the strings of an instrument played by a practised hand.' A word here and a word there, and 'she seemed to know what note each string would give out before she touched it'. But Julie made a point always of keeping up a polite tone; this was just what exasperated d'Alembert; it was just like the Hôtel de Rambouillet all over again, he grumbled.

Doubtless d'Alembert, at the summit of his fame, was a star attraction at Julie's. Permanent secretary to the Academy, he was the target of every visitor in search of academic honours. He was to be seen at every one of Julie's receptions, and as a sort of master of ceremonies he gave her all his spare time. In the end he quarrelled with Madame du Deffand, who faced him with the straight alternative: her or me.

So d'Alembert left his lodgings with the glazier's widow who had been his foster-mother, and moved into the same house as Julie. There is no doubt he was in love with her, and of course all Paris talked of their forthcoming marriage, a rumour which d'Alembert contradicted in a letter to Voltaire of 1766: 'She is worthy of a better match than me, and there is between us neither love nor intended marriage.' In the same letter he says that the gossip about their supposed love affair came from Madame du Deffand; but that 'an infamous old trull like her knows nothing about honest women, and does not believe in them'.

Was it really a question of virtue? Grimm, in his letters, speaking of d'Alembert, says: 'All Paris knows the answer he made to a fanatical admirer of his who cried out in his enthusiasm "Here is a god!"—"Come, come," says he, "A god would have begun by making himself man!"'

And Rousseau, in his *Confessions*, says: 'They lived together, in all honesty, you understand, and indeed how could anyone understand otherwise?'

However that may be, the love of d'Alembert for Julie was an unhappy one. And now the prudent, the reasonable Julie, with all her self-control, becomes a prey to passion. She falls in love with the Marquis de Mora, a Spanish grandee, who had attracted the sympathies of Voltaire by his adhesion to the anti-Jesuit party. He might even have married Julie had he not died of consumption in Spain.

While all her friends including d'Alembert were straining every nerve to console her, a new star appeared on the horizon of her affections: the Comte de Guibert, a very young officer, and an indifferent versifier who read his works in an over-emphatic style at Julie's *salon*, hoping for her patronage in a literary career. But she was fifteen years older than he, and her devouring passion embarrassed him, so he got himself appointed military attaché to the French mission at various European courts, and ended up as a quite important writer on military subjects, marrying a girl of seventeen who had a nice little fortune.

It was this last love which really burnt up Julie. In her despair she began to overdo the doses of opium which she had to take anyway for her insomnia, until in 1776 she died in the arms of d'Alembert. Her letters to her lover, as burning with passionate love as those of the Portuguese Nun, were published years later, curiously enough, by the widowed Comtesse de Guibert.

MADAME DU DEFFAND'S PASSION

Madame du Deffand admits: 'It is sheer boredom that drives me to fill the the house with guests.' Constantly making conversational capital out of the foibles of her friends, she is always straining after new friendships. And the older she grows, the more her desire for company, her curiosity, her anxiety increase. Sometimes in a letter she communicates her enthusiasm for some new acquaintance, and in the next letter cynically rejects it.

Her innate pessimism clouds her thoughts, her feelings. The thought of death appalls her. She asks herself: 'How to believe what one does not understand?' Doubts about everything, even about friendship, which she cannot do without. This doubt insinuates itself even into the most precious relationships, such as that which unites her to the charming wife of the Duc de Choiseul, a minister of Louis XV. 'You know you love me,' she writes to the Duchesse, 'though you do not *feel* it.'

But the time is coming when Madame du Deffand's letters will be not only the mirror of an uneasy world, a stormy world, but the reflection of a deeply moving personal destiny. In

October 1765 Horace Walpole, who was to occupy so large a place in her affections, arrived in Paris. He has a great liking for wit, the French quality *par excellence*, he loves the French way of making fun of everything, of treating lightly and gracefully fundamental problems. But he himself is brimming with wit. The best of himself he poured into his letters, which are masterpieces of the kind.

Walpole had been to Paris before, twenty-five years earlier, but without gaining entry to intellectual circles. At that time he criticized the rat-race of fashion and modish amusements, the French conception of honour—so different from the English version—but now he is impressed by the transformation of society. 'The women,' he writes, 'if they are not so gay as before, are better educated, and this goes to make conversation very pleasant.'

Madame du Deffand is sitting on her big, roomy armchair—the one she calls her 'barrel'. She cannot see her new visitor, Horace Walpole, but lightly brushes his face with her hand, as is her habit with people to whom she is introduced.

The next day Walpole writes to a friend: 'Old President Hénault is the Grand Pagoda at Mme du Deffand's, who is an old blind lady drunk with wit, with whom I supped last night. The old president is nearly deaf and even more advanced in senility. When he sits down to table, the mistress of the house (who was once his) asks after every dish, and who partook of it, and shouts all this information down the president's ear-trumpet.'

But soon the tone of the letters changes fundamentally. Walpole does not miss one of Madame du Deffand's suppers. He marvels at her intelligence, her long memory, the delicacy of her wit. A month after he has arrived in Paris he writes (20th November 1765): 'She corresponds with Voltaire, to whom she dictates the most piquant letters. She contradicts him boldly, has no respect for him or for anyone else, and is as independent of the clergy as of the philosophers. . . . Love and hate rule her always; her passion for her friends amounts to enthusiasm, and the desire to be loved still racks her, though of course it is not love I mean. . . .'

Not love? But how else could one describe the feelings which at sixty-eight she had for Walpole, then younger than her by twenty years? She for whom in her young days love was a mere amusement, is now a prey to passion.

A year later Walpole left Paris, but, uneasy about the fate of the old blind lady, he asked his friends to look after her and not desert to the camp of her rival, '. . . a certain Demoiselle de Lespinasse, a so-called wit, who was once the humble companion of Madame du Deffand, who has betrayed her and treated her very badly.'

In her correspondence with Walpole Madame du Deffand's passion breaks out without pause or rest. Letter after letter she dictates to her secretary, telling her far-off friend countless details of her household, of Voltaire, of the philosophers; she runs them all down: 'In your country you have no such set of ridiculous people as most our academicians are.' Finally she repudiates her own country, saying: 'I am all English' and will admit no one can write but Shakespeare. Sometimes late in the night she gropes her way to her desk and scrawls in shaky letters: 'There can be no love more tender than mine to you . . . I am ready to let myself be led like a child, forget my life back to the age of thirteen . . . you will wipe out my entire past, and I shall begin to live from the day I met you.'

Walpole's coldness irks her. 'You have one inexcusable weakness. To it you sacrifice all feeling, and bend your conduct to it. That is the fear of being laughed at. It makes you dependent on the good opinion of fools.' In fact, Walpole does often seem embarrassed and reacts to romantic utterances by cynical remarks.

But is he really as insensible towards Madame du Deffand as he makes out? In a letter to a friend, March 1766, he says: 'She is kind, affectionate, delicate and fair—so fair-minded that I find it tedious to be always going against her goodness of heart, and to be destroying the vain illusions she has about the nature of our friendship.' And later on: 'I talk to Mmes de Mirepoix, de Boufflers, de Luxembourg, for fear of loving Madame du Deffand too much. And after all, they only make me love her more.'

For all that, the old lady's passion afflicted him; there was besides the fear that their letters should be opened by indiscreet third parties. 'Am I cut out to be the hero of an epistolatory novel?' he asks indignantly. But in spite of all that, Madame du Deffand's letters get more and more exalted.

Slowly Walpole was to manage to stem the flood of her passion. Sometimes she resisted still. She called on the shade of

Madame de Sévigné, whom Walpole called his saint: 'I pray her to appease your wrath; she will tell you that she had feelings as guilty as mine, but was an honest person for all that.'

But these two creatures stand for two utterly different worlds, this woman in whom love has awakened so late and has taken entire command of her feelings, and this imperturbably cool Englishman, balanced and inimical to all excess. The dichotomy is summed up in a sentence written by Walpole to a friend: 'I do not share Madame du Deffand's opinion, that it is better to be dead than not to love, on the contrary: I think it better to be dead than to be in love.'

At last Madame du Deffand determined not to oppress him any more with her sentimental lamentations. She expressed this good resolution in the form of a song which she wrote in 1768:

Vous n'aurez plus à vous plaindre
De mon trop d'empressement.
Ouvrez mes lettres sans craindre
d'y trouver du sentiment.
Je sens, je sens
Que je peux, sans me contraindre,
Prendre un ton différent.

Resigned at last, she wrote to him: 'Let our conversation henceforward be of trifles, let us be done with love for ever, with friendship, with flirtation: let us not love each other, but still be interested in each other without departing from your principles.' The humility of this woman, customarily so proud, is infinitely more moving than her sentimental effusions.

Walpole came back to Paris in 1775. When he left again Madame du Deffand had a presentiment that this was to be their last meeting: '*Adieu.* What a sad word! Remember that you leave behind the person who loves you most, and for whom your opinion, good or bad, makes all the difference between happiness and sorrow.'

MADAME DU DEFFAND AND VOLTAIRE

Was the bond between Madame du Deffand and Voltaire ever anything more than an intellectual one? We have more than one proof of her jealousy towards the Marquise du Châtelet, if only in her portrait of the fair Émilie, who, as she said, 'tried so hard to appear what she was not, that now she does not know what she really is'. One of her remarks about Madame du Châtelet is pertinent: 'To be a celebrity, one must be talked about. And this she has achieved by becoming Voltaire's mistress . . . if she lives in the centuries to come, she will owe it to him.'

Perhaps, who knows, the rivalry between these two women was above all an intellectual one. Be that as it may, Madame du Deffand and Voltaire ceased to write to each other when the latter began to live with Madame du Châtelet, and only started again in 1749, after her death.

The letters are of unusual interest. Stimulating, fascinating, exciting, genuine documents of the period, they chronicle every event of town and Court. And we discover that not only were they matched in intelligence, but in brilliance and spontaneity Madame du Deffand excelled Voltaire.

Caustically, gracefully, she makes light of the authorities, the Academicians, with their vanities and their mutual admiration. She calls nearly all the Encyclopaedists precious pedants, tolerating only those who, like Voltaire, are avid for the truth.

At this distance of time how are we able to judge the deservedness of her mockery? The *Encyclopédie* strikes us as a miracle of scientific exposition, of clarity of thought. And we admire its contributors for their fearless struggle in favour of justice and toleration. But on the other hand, these letters from Madame du Deffand glitter so, their clear style sparkles so brightly, that we find it hard to resist siding with her. Does not the public always side with the mockers?

It seems to us in reading these letters that Madame du Deffand showed more taste for Voltaire's wit than for his pugnacious defence of equity; we find few allusions in them to his attacks on miscarriages of justice. What both had in common was fanatical devotion to the truth. Voltaire wrote to her from exile at Ferney: 'How should I not love you? You are always in search of the truth, and this is a quality rare as the truth itself. I dare say I resemble you in this; that in my heart and mind I have always sacrificed everything to what I believe to be the truth.'

Madame du Deffand is even more forthcoming. 'The search for truth is for you the universal panacea. So it is for me too, but not in the same sense as it is for you, for you think you have found it, but I think it is unattainable.'

Madame du Deffand's pessimism irks Voltaire. When she writes: 'There is only one misfortune in life, that is, being born,' he is annoyed, because he feels in this a threat to his reasons for living; so he takes refuge behind flippant, witty remarks, for he would not at any price dare follow Madame du Deffand in her desperate search for a sense of direction in life.

When she was very old Madame du Deffand was revolted by Voltaire's anti-religious fanaticism. For him, death would be nothing but a sleep, and so the sacraments were 'evil demons' serving only to remind the dying that they would never wake again. But Madame du Deffand, who understood the comfort that many derived from extreme unction, answered him: 'I think the manner of one's death proves very little . . . it needs but a stroke of imagination to decide, and we should be very foolish to restrain ourselves in our last moments.'

The old lady even went to the length of putting herself under the direction of her confessor, without losing one whit of her humour or her sarcastic wit: 'I have given up going to the play: I go to High Mass at the parish church.' Enlightened minds in Paris were disconcerted by the conversion of Madame du Deffand. Freethinkers, who had thought of her as one of themselves, felt betrayed. Voltaire tried to turn her away from ecclesiastical influence but in vain.

In a letter to Walpole she bemoans her age, which prevents her playing her part in the fascinating life of Paris. 'And yet,' she sighs, 'society has been the essence of my life.' She quotes La Rochefoucauld on the Court: 'It doesn't make one happy, but prevents one from being so elsewhere.'

In 1778, having been away thirty years, the patriarch of Ferney returned to Paris, hailed as the hero of the Calas case by all and sundry. Madame du Deffand wrote to Walpole: 'At eighty-four, he is so young as to seem immortal.'

But Voltaire was not immortal. Broken by the exertion of travel and by emotion attendant on the ceremonies in his honour he died soon after his home-coming. Was it coldness of heart or the fear of giving way to her feelings which made Madame du Deffand write to Walpole, about the death of a man with whom she had been united in friendship for half a century: 'He died of an overdose of opium which he took to kill the pain . . . and I would add, of an overdose of fame'?

For her part, cynicism remained her best defensive weapon

against ill-health and the vacuum created around her by the disappearance of her friends. She had retained all the wit and mental clarity of her youth. Old age, for her, was nothing less than calamity. Discouraged, she quoted Voltaire:

Qui de son âge n'a pas l'esprit
De son âge a tous les malheurs.

In a moving verse, written some months before her death in 1780, all her melancholy, but also all her clearsightedness, are revealed:

Il est un âge affreux, sombre et froide saison,
Ou l'homme encor s'égare et prend dans sa tristesse
Son impuissance pour sagesse
Et ses craintes pour sa raison.

Had she any presentiment of the great upheaval, the imminent annihilation of her own class? No. No echo came to her of the grumblings of rebellion, and even in the days of her youth she had been but an impassive spectator of events.

Madame du Deffand had never taken sides, had never been committed. She was never the inspirer of poets or the protectress of artists. She was less, and yet infinitely more than that: for her own century throbs and hums in her, fluid, light, intangible, indefinable, an alloy of virtue and immorality, of romantic idealization and frivolity, of an intelligence full of fantasy and a fantasy limited by intelligence.

CHAPTER FIVE

MRS MONTAGU AND THE BLUE STOCKINGS

LADIES AND GENTLEMEN

We are at Bath, in the middle of the eighteenth century when it was still the most fashionable spa in England. A Mrs Vesey, who has intellectual ambitions, meets on the promenade Mr Benjamin Stillingfleet, a wit and a man of wide learning. 'Do call on me,' she says, 'I am having a conversazione today; it is my "office of the mind", of which you will have heard.' Stillingfleet is at a loss, for he is not in full dress. What is worse, he is not wearing white silk stockings, so indispensable for all formal occasions. But Mrs Vesey is no stickler for conventions: 'Come just as you are, in your blue stockings.'

Is this story sheer invention? It may be, for there is another version of the genesis of the phrase: it lays more emphasis on the importance of Mr Stillingfleet in this circle than the above anecdote. One way or the other, it does not matter how the expression arose. Certain it is that the term 'blue-stocking parties' was born at this time, and as yet had no ironic overtones, but retained its pristine freshness.

Indeed, in England these assemblies, veritable tournaments of wit between cultured men and women, were still a surprising novelty. Up to that time 'Town' (London) and 'country' ladies had sat interminably at their whist tables, indulging in empty chatter and conversational banalities. What did these ladies know of the *salons* of Paris, where for more than a century past the problems of the day had been tackled, and where great ladies reigned over literary and philosophical coteries? They knew nothing, for scarcely a breath of these doings had been wafted over the Channel.

What, hold serious conversations in a drawing-room, expound new ideas in the presence of women? It was inconceivable in England. Burning questions were debated in clubs, in coffee houses, in taverns, and at the outset of the eighteenth century there were over eight thousand coffee-houses in London alone, all opened since 1652, though it must be admitted that in provincial towns they were much thinner on the ground. In these smelly, smoke-laden resorts the arguments of the opposition were thrashed out, the latest political happenings were commented on, pamphlets were drafted, business deals concluded, marital irregularities laughed over. The Swiss Louis de Muralt, writing in 1726, says: 'No one asks any more where So-and-so lives, but to what coffee-house he resorts.' Only the beaux, the wild young bucks, met in chocolate houses, which were socially deemed a cut above the coffee house (there were fewer of them).

Every club and every coffee house had its distinctive political complexion. But all of them had the flavour of opposition, no matter whether Box or Cox was in power. Here the Tories waxed indignant about every sort of innovation, about agrarian reform, about liberty of thought, about freedom of religion: there the Whigs grew enthusiastic about the Free Churches, even a Free Church, about the sovereignty of Parliament, about the untrammelled privileges of the mercantile classes.

In fact since the dawn of the century the middle class had triumphed. It was to set its seal not only on social life but on costume and fashion and customs. It had risen to material power with dizzying speed. It would be difficult to imagine such a middle class in any other country but England, so typical is it of that nation. It had only one barrier left to cross before attaining the quintessence of Englishness: the city man had to become a gentleman. He need not bother about blue blood or a sonorous surname, or a family tree, but he must have good manners (which probably already included the right accent, unless he were Scottish), a noble bearing, a distinguished presence: the ownership of landed property was a help. The full-fledged gentleman, a man of integrity and balance, is able to reconcile the ideal with the useful, and to combine business ability with puritanical principle, eschewing all fanaticism: even his political convictions are governed by reason.

A new ethic was about to triumph over the depravity to which puritanism had given way, in 'Town' at least, since the Restoration. The theatre is an uninhibited pornographic show. Even John Gay, with his *Beggar's Opera*, does not conceal his admiration for his hero, who is addicted to robbery with violence and grievous bodily harm. But already pamphlets and novels based on moral fundamentals are being published, such as *Gulliver's Travels* (1726), Swift's pitiless satire of the King and his minister Walpole, on Parliament and on the whole of English society. Hogarth, the leading English artist, grovels amid haunts of vice, but always with the object of drawing a moral lesson. His prints have a wide sale and demonstrate that frivolity and profligacy do not pay; they cudgel the upper-class outlook and demonstrate their calamities in *Marriage à la Mode*.

How is this new revolution, this intrusion of a new ethic into literary and artistic spheres, to be explained? Woman, and her quite new social status, is the cause. English journalists and novelists who hitherto had written solely for men, now discover the existence of a female public. And those who hereafter aim at this public adopt a changed style and accent: scepticism and cynicism give way to the human, not to say the sentimental, touch. And even humour, hitherto coarse, aggressive, pitiless, is tamed: it becomes positively smooth.

Virtue is the order of the day, virtue above all. Countless pedagogic guides preach it. Novelists edify their lady readers by showing its advantages. And for the first time, too, the middle-class heroine begins to figure in English literature. Spotless protagonist of the novel, she is contrasted with the woman of the world, the smart lady surrounded by gallants. The outlines of the ideal Englishwoman emerge: not at all emancipated, but morally independent, endowed with high human qualities.

This figure of the perfect Englishwoman was a totally masculine creation. But it must be said that her creators wanted her to be colourless, timid, and as little intellectual as possible. She may be well schooled, know several languages, but she must not make much of it, must not appear the 'learned lady'. Lord Chesterfield, in his *Letters to his Son*, says that a man of sense only trifles with women, as he does a sprightly forward child, but neither consults them about nor trusts them with serious matters.*

However, little by little, these manuals of feminine propriety disappear. Puritanism abandons its bellicose stance, it softens and becomes sociable, even socially acceptable. So that the

* Thus also Lord Lyttelton, in *Advice to a Lady:*

For wit like wine intoxicates the brain
Too strong for feebld women to sustain.

things of the mind, learning and letters, are no longer forbidden ground to women. On the contrary, they are expected to air their knowledge, even make a show of it. Cosmopolitanism contributes to this, for some of the great minds, historians and philosophers such as Hume, Robertson, Gibbon, Horace Walpole, having crossed the Channel and been guests in the *salons* of Paris, return to reveal to the English the glories of the great ladies of France.

The mid-century saw in England prodigious cultural upsurge, in which for the first time women took part. Social life rose to heights unknown before then. At social gatherings where the new urbanity allows the co-existence of directly opposed tendencies, the celebrities of the day meet the women of intellect, the 'Blue-Stocking Ladies' (who do not themselves wear blue stockings).

The immense wealth which commerce and industry have brought form a material basis on which a society can be built up with a sense of the beautiful and an ideal of perfection. Architecture, furniture such as Chippendale's, Wedgwood pottery, are only a few examples. This is one of the peak periods of English art, with the Adam brothers, Reynolds, Gainsborough, Romney.

The artist, like the woman, will derive his benefit from the sudden rise of the mercantile class. He can behave as an equal in the houses of the nobility and gentry. Portraits by Gainsborough and Reynolds reflect the familiarity of the artist with his model, and much more vividly than the accounts of historians impart to us the very texture of society.

From the walls of the National Portrait Gallery ladies and gentlemen look out on us at a much closer range than do their French contemporaries, the *grands seigneurs* of the old régime. Members of Parliament, noblemen and squires, actors and actresses, Blue-Stocking ladies, all have the same presence, the same aristocratic bearing, showing that they no longer belong to a closed caste but are part of a whole society of mental quality.

THE IGNORAMUS OF LOVE

Elizabeth Robinson seemed born to be Queen of the Blue Stockings. Brought up by a vastly learned grandfather, who was able to teach her a certain virtuosity of expression, surrounded by admirers, she had from early youth been ambitious to play her part in the society of York, where she was born. She lived for candlelight, for elegant dresses, for balls and for routs.

Short, almost squat, her blue eyes sparkling with life and wit; so her contemporaries describe her. She was called Fidget by her friends, having earned the nickname by her liveliness and ceaseless activity.

But Fidget knew what she wanted. The letters which this young girl wrote to her confidential friend the Duchess of Portland, who was six years older, are very revealing. There is not much heart, plenty of brain, and a certain lack of spontaneity. At barely twenty years old she juggles with Latin and Greek quotations, discourses sagely on futilities, strains after poetic effects. Comparison of these letters with those written by the same hand in maturity allows us to gauge what a will of iron can achieve. A personal colouring replaces pale reflections, the flavour of wit replaces the commonplace, deep knowledge instead of counterfeit learning.

When she was still very young Elizabeth conceived the model of her ideal husband: intelligent enough to direct her, witty enough to keep her amused, handsome enough to please her, not without enough humour to excuse her faults, and rich enough to assure material comfort. 'I am like Pygmalion,' she writes to the Duchess, 'in love with a picture of my own drawing—but I never saw an original like it in my life.'

She is very fond of repeating 'sentiment, a dangerous guide'. So much cold intelligence, such poise, so much reserve are rather forbidding, and what she called her virtue we should call frigidity today. We should not be far from the truth, for Mrs Chapone, a friend of hers among the Blue Stockings, called her 'the Ignoramus in Love' forty years later.

When she was twenty-two she chose her own husband; that Mr Montagu whom she married in 1742, when he was forty-two. He was a wealthy coal-owner, an amateur mathematician, a moderate Whig in politics, living a blameless life and respected by all. The day after her wedding she wrote to the Duchess of Portland that she had behaved well during the ceremony and had not cried even when the benediction was pronounced—'and yet my mind was in no mirthful mood'.

The Montagus lead a typically English upper-class life,

spending the winter in London and the summer on their estate in Berkshire, far from the coal mines. It was at their Berkshire place that their son was born, only to die at eighteen months old, and Elizabeth never bore another child.

Mrs Montagu's breakfasts and her elegant afternoon at-homes usher in the Blue-Stocking era. And since, for the Perfect Lady (which was not yet a term of mockery), an impeccable turnout, faultless behaviour and a flawless education were indispensable, one can well imagine how many proud virtues were dried out daily, like flowers pressed between the leaves of a book. But in fact this was not to happen for another fifty years yet.

To begin with, the meetings of the Blue Stockings had no tinge of pedantry. Liveliness and liberty, and above all a great simplicity, were the rule there. Madame du Boccage, whose Paris *salon* was on a par with that of Madame du Deffand, came to London in 1750. What a different world, what a radical disparity, between the societies of London and Paris!

'Great as is the luxury in the homes of the English,' she writes, 'they are a hundred years behind us and the rest of Europe in all that they imitate.' She admits that a woman can become Queen of England in her own right, but she goes on: 'The women wear no make-up and are all tight-laced as once they were in France; so that, in Court dress and pinched in at the waist, they look like portraits of our grandmothers at Marly.'

Madame du Boccage describes thus a breakfast at Mrs Montagu's, whom she calls 'Mylady Montaigue': 'We breakfasted today in a room hung with Chinese hand-painted paper, and furnished with the prettiest Chinese pieces: a long table covered with a diaphanous cloth, on which a thousand shining vessels offered coffee, chocolate, cream, biscuits, butter, various kinds of toast, together with delicious tea . . . which the lady of the house herself poured out.'

Mrs Montagu's taste was too good not to recognize the aesthetic blunders that a past generation had committed. In a letter of 1752 she makes fun of her Chinese room, swarming with people from eleven in the forenoon to eleven in the evening. She finds it crude and barbaric, of dubious ostentation, and likes to compare it to a Hindu temple (of course she has never seen a Hindu temple) with its Chinese pictures painted on gauze, its fan-backed bamboo chairs, and its pagodas.

Now fifteen years have passed, a whole chapter in the evolution of taste to which the drawing-rooms at Mrs Montagu's, transformed and rejuvenated, bear witness. This is just the moment for an elegant urbanity to assert itself, for a social *élite* to create a comfortable and elegant setting for its home life. Mrs Montagu, who is always up to date, consults the fashionable architect Robert Adam. He transforms the interior of her house in Hill Street, Mayfair, tearing down and rebuilding ceilings, fireplaces, doorways, in a fantastic yet harmonious style—'the whole pretty enough to make me a thousand enemies', as she writes in 1765.

Mr Montagu's friends are not unaware of her failings, but they admire her. Flatterers even ascribe genius to her. Her prestige is great, her influence in Blue-Stocking circles considerable. To be sure, she has nothing like the glittering wit of Madame du Deffand, seemingly nothing like the charm of the great ladies of Paris. Her letters are often didactic and moralizing in tone and she never misses the chance of riddling with irony the love affairs of the French marquises and the importance which dramatic authors, in France, attach to love. But when all is said and done, Mrs Montagu is an exceptional woman, both for the period and for her country. Her bold convictions, her clear understanding, her strong personality fascinated and drew into her circle thinkers and artists such as Johnson, Burke, Hume, Garrick and Reynolds.

'In body a saint, in mind a great sinner.' It was thus that later she drew her own portrait. However, little stories about her private life proliferated. Horace Walpole, a connoisseur of scandal, was not slow to repeat them. What a strange personality, attractive and repellant by turns, had this son of the famous chancellor Robert Walpole. Witty, fanciful, malicious, a brilliant letter-writer, Horace Walpole delighted in combining the most contradictory characteristics, now playing the virtuous pedant, now the rake, now the disillusioned man of the world. He was quite capable of betraying a friend or ruining a friendship, if it afforded the opportunity to turn some elegant phrases.

Mrs Montagu was among the victims of his tittle-tattle. He wrote to George Montagu, the eminent scholar: 'I was diverted with the story of a lord and a lady who bears your name: her postillion, a lad of fifteen, said, "I am not such a child but I can guess something. Whenever Lord Lyttelton comes to see my lady, she orders the porter to let in nobody else, and they call for pens and ink, and say, they are going to write history."'

This was slander, for in fact they were just writing. Not long after, in 1760, *Dialogues of the Dead* came out under Lyttelton's name. It would perhaps have attracted little notice had it not been for the last three dialogues which Lyttelton says in his preface are not by his own hand, for the whole is somewhat mediocre. In fact Mrs Montagu wrote the last three.

But no one is safe from calumny. People even gossiped about the good understanding that she enjoyed with William Pulteney, Earl of Bath, a prominent political figure who at this time was eighty to her forty years of age. Mrs Montagu takes up the cudgels: 'I am ready to declare to the whole world that I never saw anything that I could love, esteem and honour even to veneration as I do my Lord Bath; if they can prove it to be a sin or shame to love the most amiable and admire the most noble virtues and talents, let them put as much sin and shame to my account as they please.'

A certain Dr Monsey, physician to Chelsea Hospital, a grotesque character who was the clown of Blue-Stocking society, was old too when he wrote to Mrs Montagu, then in the country, what can only be described as love letters. She speaks of one to Stillingfleet, in a letter of 1757: 'Dr Monsey is fallen desperately in love with me and I more passionately in love with him. We have said so many tender things to each other by the post that at last we thought it better to sigh in soft dialogues. . . .' But every time Dr Monsey is due to come, one of his grandchildren falls ill, and Mrs Montagu decides to fall out of love with this grandfather: 'but when we get to Elysium, all the lovers who wander in the myrtle groves there will throw garlands at our feet.'

Mr Montagu died in 1775, bequeathing his immense fortune to his wife, coal mines, estates and all. She shortly proved herself a very competent general manager of these undertakings, administering the industrial side as well as cleverly running the estates. As the patroness of the miners—'Good souls, men and women, very apt to get drunk'—she now and again distributes rations to their poor children—'some cheap rice, skim milk and coarse beef.'

With the growing power derived from her riches, Mrs Montagu's intellectual ambitions also grew. Soon they broadened to the point where we see her surrounded by leading scientific and literary personalities, keeping up a regular correspondence with them. Her letters are undoubtedly of high quality; published in four volumes some years after her death, they give an interesting glimpse of her era, as well as pleasure in the reading. In the end, her wish was to come true; she became an author herself, a genuine literary lady. Though queen in her own domain, she was not the only one to qualify for the honourable title of Blue Stocking.

THE OTHER BLUE STOCKINGS

Conversaziones are all the fashion. What lady of the least wit and learning would not banish the card table from her drawing-room? Even in the country, ladies' invitation cards read: '. . . to take tea and walk in the park.' And these walks in the park implied conversation, discussion of some interesting subject. But was it enough to call oneself a Blue Stocking? Far from it; the way to this exalted rank lay through a feminine *élite* of lofty ambitions, if not some pretension to posthumous fame.

Of such was Mrs Vesey. Walpole, catty as ever, called her a collector of celebrities and of pretenders to fame. But above all Mrs Vesey was a gifted hostess. What she aimed at was to make other people's talents shine, keep them in good humour, so that even Mrs Montagu, full of admiration for the magic formula which enabled Mrs Vesey to create an atmosphere of harmony out of the most incompatible elements, questioned her about the jostling throng of young bucks and old cits, military men and rebels, lords and scholars, who filled the Vesey reception rooms. 'In my house,' Mrs Montagu exclaimed, 'five or six men would have been called out, there would have been several lawsuits and mortal hatreds without number.'

With her fanatical contempt for protocol, Mrs Vesey eschewed the conventional circular arrangement of furniture, and strewed her rooms with chairs and settees placed haphazardly. Hard of hearing, trailing a chair behind her, she fluttered from one group to another; 'Why is nobody talking this evening? I don't hear a single word!' Gentle and kind, she forgave her huband his many infidelities. But was not this common form at the time? The German writer, C. P. Moritz, was astonished during his visit to

England in 1782, and says: 'English women are so charitable that they do not scruple to invite their husbands' mistresses to their table.' For all that, the sensitive Mrs Vesey's grief resulted in a long-standing nervous depression, of which the deafness may have been a psychosomatic symptom.

Such conjugal misfortune ran no risk of complicating Elizabeth Carter's career. Her fairy godmother had not endowed her with any natural talents. But she made up for this by her tenacity, her zeal. As a young girl she had spent long nights sustained by tea and snuff, learning languages both ancient and modern. She achieved a certain celebrity by her translation of Epictetus. More than that, she was very feminine, gay, gracious, not at all pedantic. Here is what Dr Johnson thought of her: 'Sir, a man would rather have a good dinner than a woman that was master of the Greek. My old friend Miss Carter could make a pudding as well as translate Epictetus from the Greek.'

Nevertheless Miss Carter's femininity could not come to its full flowering in the society of England. But in 1763, no sooner had she landed in France in company with the Montagus, than the obstacles melted away. 'With the same facility with which she translated Epictetus from the Greek, she translates her native timidity into French airs and French modes. She has bought robes trimmed with *blond* and *soucidenton*, bouquets. Instead of translating the memorable things of Socrates, you may expect a lively and spirited version of les amours et amourettes du Marquis de . . .' wrote Mrs Montagu in a letter to Mrs Vesey.

What shall we say of the dogged persistency on Mrs Chapone's part which rewarded her with the rank of Blue-Stocking lady? Barely twenty-two years of age, she had already digested the ten volumes of *Cyrus the Great* and no doubt a great number of the maxims of morality which stud the pages of Mrs Chapone's *Letters to a Young Lady on the Improvement of the Mind* are borrowed from Mademoiselle de Scudéry; at any rate, her book was many times reprinted and translated into many languages.

These Blue-Stocking ladies had one thing in common: all were indefatigable correspondents and diarists. As witness Mrs Delany. Her memoirs run to no less than six volumes. In her youth she had known Swift and Pope, about whom she had a store of amusing reminiscences. Happy were the Blue Stockings

A FÊTE AT THE COURT OF BURGUNDY, or 'The Garden of Love of Philip the Good', Duke of Burgundy.
French School (fifteenth century); Versailles. *Photo: Archives-Photographiques*

THE COURT OF ISABELLA D'ESTE, or 'The Court of the Muses'. Painting by Lorenzo Costa; the Louvre. *Photo: Giraudon*

THE CASTLE OF MANTUA. *Photo: Alinari-Giraudon*

MADAME GEOFFRIN.
Painting by Jean Chardin; Musée Fabre, Montpellier.
Photo: Bulloz

A READING IN A SALON; first half of the eighteenth century.
Painting by J.-F. de Troy; private collection.
Photo: Giraudon

MADAME DU DEFFAND.
Engraving after a drawing by Louis Carmontelle. *Photo: Roger-Viollet*

MRS. ELIZABETH MONTAGU.
Engraving by J. T. Smith after a portrait by Reynolds.
Photo: Ullstein

RAHEL VARNHAGEN.
From a drawing by
Wilhelm Hensel, 1822.
Photo: Ullstein

CRISTINA DE BELGIOJOSO.
Painting by Charles Lehmann, 1841.
Palazzo Visconti d'Aragona, Milan. *Photo: Bulloz*

JULIETTE ADAM.
Painting by Eugène Charpentier.
Photo: Archives-Photographiques

A SOIRÉE IN 1878.
Painting by Jean Béraud; Musée Carnavalet.
Photo: Hachette. © *by S.P.A.D.E.M. Paris* 1969

in their day, never pressed for time as we are, and Mrs Delany had time between her letter-writing and journal entires to cut out endless floral paper patterns.

Among all the letters, all the diaries, there is so little that reveals to us the private life of a Blue Stocking. Were they flirtatious, capricious, even in love, ever rivals in love? To be sure, they were rivals in other respects, but in a restrained and measured way. No hateful jealousy is apparent from their letters, the virulence of a Madame du Deffand is nowhere apparent, as when she attacked her rival Mademoiselle de Lespinasse. English good breeding, how it tempered their excesses, damped down their violence, even reducing feminine coquetry to the indispensable minimum.

Never overstep the limits is the advice of the Blue Stockings. Mrs Thrale (Piozzi) who was herself a Blue, as they came to be called, and a woman of letters in her own modest right, may have passed the allowable limits. For after the death of her husband she married an Italian singer. When word of this came to her through the Blue Stocking circle Mrs Montagu was indignant: Mrs Thrale of all people, one of the most promising recruits to her set! With his wife's money Piozzi bought himself an estate in Italy. Let her stay there, let her weep out the rest of her days in Italy! But Mrs Piozzi weeps not at all; on the contrary, her letters are brimming with joy. So that all of a sudden Mrs Montagu finds the style of these letters somewhat vulgar. But then, she rather looked askance at every marriage based on emotion and not dictated by reason. 'I own it astonishes me,' she writes, 'when I hear two people voluntarily and in their own suggestion entering into a bargain for perhaps fifty years cohabitation. I am so much of Colman's advice that the end of a feast is better than the beginning of a fray, that I weep more at a wedding than a funeral.'

But soon the two youngest members of the set, Fanny Burney and Hannah More, had surpassed the other ladies in fame. Samuel Johnson was delighted to see Mrs Montagu supplanted by a young competitor, and wrote to Fanny Burney in 1778: 'Down with her, Burney! Spare her not, attack her, fight her, and down with her at once! You are a rising wit, and she is at the top.'

But Fanny is generous. The rivalry means little to her. From their first meeting a lasting friendship was established between the two women. Besides, Fanny Burney was not lacking in clear-sightedness. Of course she valued the sure judgment of Mrs Montagu, her critical faculties, her sparkling conversation. But she found her estimable rather than likeable, for she lacked, as she herself put it, 'the gift of loving'.

Fanny Burney published her novel *Evelina* anonymously in 1778, for that was then the only decent thing for a lady author to do. The book was a triumph. No novel had had such success since the publication of Richardson's *Clarissa*. Fanny, too, wrote her memoirs. And they are no trifle; they run to seven volumes. Drawn up in a lively style, often in dialogue, they are not without interest, especially in those passages dealing with the unhappy period when Fanny was serving in boredom at Windsor as second Keeper of the Robes to Queen Charlotte.

In 1793 Fanny married Monsieur d'Arblay, a French émigré. This was a terribly romantic thing to do, or so Mrs Montagu thought. To marry a gentleman devoid alike of fortune and fatherland! But alas, Fanny was not the only one to have such extravagant ideas. Mrs Montagu is disturbed: 'The last events in France make me sorry to have English blood mixed with French.'

And now the youngest of the Blue Stockings, Hannah More, the pride and joy of the set, a dramatist, novelist, well known also for her didactic writings and by her foundation of an educational establishment for young ladies.

In order to cheer up Mrs Vesey, the unhappy wife of a fly-by-night husband, and suffering, as we have seen, from nervous depression, Hannah composed in 1788 a long poem which was to be published as a broadsheet, called *The Bas Bleu, or Conversation*. For all who are interested in the Blue Stockings it is entirely satisfying; it will tell them, in easy verse, all they wish to know: how, almost spontaneously, cultured ladies banned cards from their tables, and replaced them by witty conversation; how ideas were exchanged between intellectual ladies and men of worth, and how this helped to free English society from its splendid isolation, in the end conferring on it a European reputation.

'At length the mental shades decline,
Colloquial wit begins to shine.
Genius prevails, and Conversation
Emerges into Reformation.'

The Bas-Bleu

LITERARY LADY

'I wasted the first half of my life in feminine frivolities and domestic trivialities.' Thus Mrs Montagu, at the age of thirty-seven, passed judgment on the years of her youth.

Three years later her three dialogues in Lord Lyttelton's work, were published. Did she, in these three dialogues, attempt a caricature of her own youth? A flirtatious smart woman, Mrs Modish, due to be fetched by Mercury to the Beyond, keeps putting him off because she has so many engagements to fill—dinners, theatres, cards, parties. . . . But at the end of the season she is quite ready to go with him, thinking the Elysian Fields less boring than country-house life in England.

Mrs Montagu exults in a letter to Miss Carter: 'At last I may become an author in form.' In fact she has some rave notices. But unfortunately other opinions are voiced. Horace Walpole criticizes the dialogues sharply, calling them *Dead Dialogues*. Johnson discredits them for ever; he called them foolishness.

Mrs Montagu is concerned. Johnson's verdict plunged her into bitter sadness. For Dr Samuel Johnson is not just any critic. All the intellectual life of the day clustered round him. In the Blue-Stocking set, every word that fell from the lips of Johnson was as gospel. He it was who set the standard of literary values. Big, burly, imposing and rough, full of prejudice, bull-headed, mercilessly frank, he was also charitable and large-hearted. Also formidably grubby. Lady Hawkins in her memoirs says that when she was a child her father used to punish her by saying: 'I'll take you to Dr Johnson this evening.'

From 1763, Boswell faithfully notes every one of his sayings, his ideas, his meditations, rendering the passionate sincerity of his criticisms as well as the narrowness of his ideas. For Johnson was not at all indulgent: he abominates every imperfection, he detests all Whigs—'the Devil was the first Whig'—and he loathes Rousseau, 'a rascal who ought to be hunted out of society'.

This same Johnson, friend of the Blue Stockings, is strictly anti-feminist, in conformity with his conservative ideas. He even denies woman the right to paint portraits. Would it not be indecent in her to draw a man's features? Ascetic, of fastidious morals, he gave up going to the theatre, as he told Garrick, in order not to see the breasts of the actresses or their white silk stockings.

In society it is Johnson, and always Johnson alone, who dominates the conversation. Many are the letters which show him in his pulpit, holding forth at the tea-table, the uncrowned, uncontested monarch of the literary realm. Mrs Montagu, like all the others, is subject to his rule. And therefore his strict verdict on her first literary effort was all the more painful to her. It was followed by an estrangement which culminated in Dr Johnson's forgetting an invitation to dinner with her. Later, when they met again in society, they sat at opposite ends of the room, setting up altar against altar, as Walpole said.

ENTER VOLTAIRE

Mrs Montagu did not stop at these first literary attempts: she was of a bellicose nature, full of patriotic feeling, and soon found an enemy to attack. This was Voltaire, the target of her pamphlet which appeared in 1769. It was published anonymously at the author's expense, under the title *An Essay on the Writings and Genius of Shakespeare . . . with Some Remarks upon the Misrepresentation of Mon. de Voltaire.*

Who would have thought that this apparently unimportant event would have consequences in the field of international politics? The reason was that Mrs Montagu's essay was strongly tinged with chauvinism. So is the tone of his criticism where Voltaire joins issue with Shakespeare: 'If the English had made prizes of fewer of our ships,' he says, 'I should have treated the creator of their theatre more indulgently.' No doubt he had his tongue in his cheek.

Undoubtedly Voltaire did not fail to recognize Shakespeare's genius. 'His genius was full of strength and exuberance, containing much of the natural and the sublime,' but, he adds, 'without the slightest spark of good taste.' Voltaire even maintained that Shakespeare had been the ruin of the English theatre. And what a lot of coarse, even obscene, passages! What a difference between Shakespeare and their Corneille, who 'makes all his heroes speak with a truly noble eloquence', who respected the unity of time, of place and of action; whereas Shakespeare 'saw fit to change the scene of action at every fall of the curtain, and to pile up thirty or forty actions one on the other, so that a single play can cover the space of twenty-five years'.

Naturally, Mrs Montagu's regard for Shakespeare was not unbounded, in which respect she conformed to contemporary opinions. Had Shakespeare lived in the country and the age of Sophocles,' she exclaims, 'what a poet he would have been!' To be sure, greater intellects than hers, such as Pope and Johnson, had expressed similar opinions. But Mrs Montagu cast them in much more lively form.

But for Voltaire to attack Shakespeare was too much, too wounding to Mrs Montagu's national pride. And therefore she did not confine herself to a counter-attack on Voltaire alone; she sought to discredit, in glorifying Shakespeare, the great French dramatists such as Corneille and Racine. How far they fall below the standard of the noble English muse! Corneille's pathetic characters lack life and animation, like Roman statues! Besides, does he not change antique heroes into French courtiers?

Once in action, Mrs Montagu passes to the attack. No, she does not care for Voltaire, 'That impertinent Frenchman'. She does not like either his private life or his freethinking ways, his scepticism or his 'detestable' *Candide*. As for his tragedy, *L'Orphelin de Chine*, it is fit only to burn! Oh, if only English poets could drive Voltaire out of Paradise in the same way as the British army had dislodged the French from North America! That these creatures should dare to criticize Shakespeare, the favoured child of fancy!

But Mrs Montagu does not confine herself to attacking. She makes a serious critical analysis of Voltaire's translation of *Julius Caesar*, points out the clumsy phrases which replace the subtle thoughts of Shakespeare, lays bare some false interpretations and the too-obvious recourse to the dictionary.

The publication of this essay made a great stir. But who was the author? Mrs Montagu wrote in a letter to her husband: 'It is whispered in Town that I am the author.' Investigations were set on foot, and the publisher questioned without result. At last it turned out that Stillingfleet had read the proofs. And from him to Mrs Montagu was but a short step.

The impression of one thousand copies sold out in a few months. Several reprints appeared in later years, but now under the author's own name, and there was to be a French translation.

Meanwhile, in France, something happened to put a spark to the powder-keg. Early in 1776 Letourneur's translation of the complete works of Shakespeare into French was published. No sooner had the first volume come out, than a storm of xenophobic indignation blew up. Voltaire thundered: a rogue who tries to present English clowns in the place of such as Corneille and Racine should stand in the pillory of Parnassus! Competition with native Gallic wits, indeed! Who would dream of offering to an audience so fine and delicate as that of the French race an author who turns the aristotelian rules upside down, and takes his heroes from the dregs of society?

But why should Voltaire, who had himself written translations of Shakespeare be so angry? Because all of a sudden the French public had found out just how much their national genius had borrowed from Shakespeare. They are now able to recognize what Voltaire's Osman owed to Othello, his Zaïre to Desdemona. And that great and moving scene from *La Mort de César* . . . did it not bear a strange resemblance to the Forum scene in *Julius Caesar*?

Grimm wrote, in a letter of 1776: 'The faithful at Ferney have not been able to read without indignation a work which will tell all France of the admirable skill with which M. de Voltaire has been able to assimilate the virtues of Shakespeare, and of the less admirable lack of good faith in which he has later seen fit to translate him.' More than hinting at plagiarism.

Three months later Grimm was to lament the Anglo-French quarrel; for up to then, such perfect harmony had reigned! The French esteemed English philosophers, we their gastronomes. They translated our novels, we their dramas. And if young English milords ruined themselves for the sake of Parisian opera singers, young French dukes went bankrupt over English racehorses. But now a storm rages over Shakespeare in French. Voltaire attacks Shakespeare, and Mrs Montagu's defence of her hero is to appear in French

Even at that day, the Channel was not wide. In a few days rumours were hawked from the Continent to the island, and from the island back to the Continent. Mrs Montagu learns that Voltaire is planning his counter-attack, which is to have an official public reading, for August. She loses no time in packing her bags and goes aboard the Channel packet.

MRS MONTAGU IN FRANCE

Mrs Montagu remains the great lady, thoroughly English and patriotic as always, in France as everywhere. Her Berlin passes through Amiens, where she believes the cathedral to be the work of English builders and is unsparing of her enthusiasm for this, the richest, the greatest, the most marvellous church that ever was seen.

Her letters are a mass of prejudice, of insularity. From the bedbugs in the hotel at Paris to the dirt and stink of its streets, the poorly clad people, the lack of goods in the shops, all is due in her estimation to the French political system, the dictatorship of the Court. Ah, it is only when we Britons are abroad that we can form a just appreciation of our British Constitution, with its judicious and moral principles! In France, this land of slavery, for example, one looks in vain for marital fidelity, parental care, filial piety. Thus sadly she writes.

Soon, however, Mrs Montagu's tone changes. Having set herself up in a nice flat at Chaillot, she plays hostess to some of the leading intellects, and is asked out in turn. Her Essay has been only partially translated into French, but already her name is known, and the compliments she receives serve to reconcile her to France. Lastly, she finds the rain of Paris preferable to dripping days in England.

She takes on a complete retinue of servants, including liveried footmen—'no comparison with our servants, who function like clockwork', with one exception—her excellent cook, so skilful that she risks inviting M. de Buffon and other members of the Academy to dinner.

For the present Mrs Montagu has entirely adopted the French style of life. In France, it is a mark of distinction to use rouge, and the effect on her is instantaneous—'I look as if I had scarlet fever.' She buys as many shoes 'as a millipede could not wear out in seven years' and hats enough and to spare for Hydra.

In her coach and six she went to call on Madame Geoffrin, now very old, as well as on that witty Madame du Deffand, 'Walpole's passion', now old too and blind, but so gay and lively that she might as well have been eighteen. On the very day of that visit Madame du Deffand told Walpole in a letter her impressions of 'la dame de Montagu'. She 'quite likes her, her conversation is laborious because she speaks our language with difficulty. But she is very polite, and did not attempt to play the schoolmistress with me.'

Zaïre is running at the theatre, and Mrs Montagu takes the opportunity to see Lekain in the part of Osman—that character so handily borrowed by Voltaire after the model of Othello. The lady is outraged by his performance; he bellows as fiercely as the hero of any bullfight! 'People of real taste seem convinced of the false taste prevalent in their tragedies.'

Besides, she adds in the same letter, the fear that people have of Voltaire is quite ridiculous. All the wits tell the most abominable stories about him, and yet everyone courts his favour.

On 19th August 1776 the great hall of the Académie is not large enough to contain the assembled company; all fashionable Paris, many English people, including the ambassador and of course Mrs Montagu. D'Alembert rises to read Voltaire's *Letter to the French Academy*, a defensive document of rare skill which passes imperceptibly from the defensive to the offensive. A certain sector of the English nation, says Voltaire, recently put up a temple to their famous actor-playwright, and some French people have strained themselves to the same pitch of enthusiasm. Well, have we not a Parisian imitation of the Thames-side Vauxhall? Do we not say 'roastbeef' for *roti de boeuf*? Do we not even boast of having eaten a 'roastbeef de mouton'? All of which is fashionable foolery. Voltaire well knew that this kind of Franglais was as pretentiously idiotic as the correspondingly gallicized English, but Voltaire himself had for long been trying to make known to his countrymen such English poets and thinkers as Pope, Dryden, Milton, Shakespeare . . . had he not translated *Julius Caesar*? And now here is an English lady accusing him of having rendered some words badly, although he was the first of all Frenchmen to make a study of the English language. As for comparing Shakespeare with Corneille and Racine, respect is paid to the opinions of the estimable Mrs Montagu of London, and her proper patriotic feelings. She prefers Shakespeare to the authors of *Iphigénie* and *Athalie*, *Polyeucte* and *Cinna*. She finds fault with Corneille's plays; certainly her criticism is not without foundation; but what a world of difference between the mistakes of Corneille in some of his plays and those of Shakespeare throughout his entire works!

Madame du Deffand wrote to Walpole: 'Madame de

Montagu behaved very well at the Academy; she never gave way to temper. She's a very reasonable woman, boring no doubt, but good-hearted and very civil.'

What self-control! For on the evening of that memorable session Mrs Montagu wrote to her sister that 'If Harlequin had been cutting his capers in front of the statue of Caesar or Alexander the Great, I could not have been more indignant than in listening to this paper of Voltaire.'

LUXURY AND DECADENCE

As the years went by, Mrs Montagu's pretensions broadened. The house in Hill Street was not smart enough. She had a regular palace built in Portman Square, to which she moved in 1782. Of course she conformed to the current architectural vogue for the classical, and commissioned James ('Athenian') Stuart, an antiquary as well as an architect. The result was all she could have wished, above all the grand salon with its colossal proportions and Palladian columns, ceilings by Angelica Kauffmann. The new house was the talk of London. Hardly had it been finished when hundreds of Londoners flocked to admire it. Mrs Montagu swelled with pride. But nothing delighted her so much as her Feather Room, the walls of which were entirely lined with the plumage of domestic and exotic fowls, collected by her over many years. Her happiness was complete when the poet Cowper glorified this room in a long poem:

'The birds cut off their every hue
To dress a room for Montagu.'

The eighties brought a new fashion, for late-night teas. Mrs Montagu of course was among the first to give them. They saddened Hannah More: 'Of all nations the English are the most foolish! How can one be at one's best, and witty as well, if two hours after a rich dinner one must partake of buttered muffins?'

The company at Mrs Montagu's becomes more and more fashionable, until one day Queen Charlotte in person appears at one of her gatherings. Mrs Montagu is in ecstasy: 'No pen can describe, no paper contain my joy. Her Majesty has even admired my Feather Room!'

Such a social success was bound to attract the mockery of

jealous rivals. Richard Cumberland, who had been Mrs Montagu's guest, published an article in the *Observer*: 'Vanessa' —so he calls his hostess—'in the centre . . . sits like the statue of the Athenian Minerva, incensed with the breath of philosophers, poets, painters, orators. She shows favour to all kinds of genius, from the manufacturer of toothpicks to the author of an epic poem, she generously opens her doors and her purse to all the sons of science and art.'

But Cumberland takes exception to all the guests and his article is one vast caricature of the Blue-Stocking set. A wounding caricature, it is true, but could it touch the queen of the Blue Stockings? And anyway, who was Cumberland? A scribbler, a botcher of melodramas, jealous of other people's success, who was known to have forbidden his children to laugh at the first night of Sheridan's *School for Scandal*! Sheridan knew all about it, and wrote: 'He ought to have laughed at my comedy, for I laughed heartily at his tragedy.'

The huge colonnaded salon of Mrs Montagu's house was soon too small to hold the crowd of guests, which got smarter and smarter. The Blue Stockings lament. Walpole brings his lively irony into play to describe this blue-blooded mob, mingled with intellectuals and artists. The 'macaronies' appear here: successors to the beaux, precursors of the dandies, affected, sophisticated, dressed in skin-tight suits, with delicately pleated shirts, they surpass in elegance the most fashionable ladies.

Alas, Mrs Montagu is growing old. Her letters betray the alteration in her spirits, and she is no longer able to perceive the significance of events. Franklin, she writes ironically, has gone to Paris to electrify the American mission there. The first ascent of Montgolfier's balloon in England is for her just a game for grown-up (if not senile) children—'but we are not so eager for new playthings as our lively neighbours in France. There is unrest in France'—this letter must have been written in 1788—'and I cannot foresee the outcome. The spirit of liberty which they have imported from America will be beat up in the froth of remonstrances and satires, rather than have any solid effect!'

When the Bastille was taken in July 1789, Mrs Montagu was outraged. And yet, hardly thirteen years earlier, she had been indignant at the despotism of the old régime. But now she sees in the uprising of the French middle class nothing but a mutiny of market stallholders. And even in England, she laments, there are women who envy their fame!

She boasts of her friendship with Edmund Burke, once a Liberal, now standard-bearer of the whole anti-revolutionary faction in Europe; thus she sings the praises of his pamphlet against the French Revolution (1790); she thinks it marvellous, perfect, incomparable. And when Thomas Paine, everywhere in the forefront where freedom's battles are fought, answers Burke in his famous *Rights of Man*, Mrs Montagu finds room for him among her hates.

Mrs Montagu's world is shrinking. For her now the only reality is her house in Portman Square, stuffed with gold, crammed with fashion. Her vision is dimmed, new values escape her. In 1798, two years before her death, her friends describe her as tired and worn-out. Nevertheless she is still busy rallying the Blue Stockings around her.

In 1800 Fanny d'Arblay, formerly Burney, laments: 'How is Blue Club cut up! All such society as that we formerly belonged to and enjoyed, being positively over. . . .'

Indeed the tale is done. The Blue-Stocking set is breaking up, and those drawing-rooms where pleasant conversation had risen to the heights of cultivation and wit, are stuck fast in a world of pedagogues and premature suffragettes.

So it came about that the epithet Blue Stocking, once a symbol of fame, suffered a sea-change, and became a laughing-stock.

CHAPTER SIX

RAHEL VARNHAGEN, 'THE SOUL OF ROMANTICISM'

THE NEW CREED

'You are the soul of romanticism,' wrote Gentz in 1830 to Rahel Varnhagen, 'and you were so before the word was invented.'

She had been born Rahel Levin. As a Jewess freed from the spiritual embrace of the ghetto, as a German in an oppressed Germany, as a woman at a time and at a place where women were still being denied their share of daylight, she was to become a torchbearer.

Since in her struggle and contradiction raged, since she was at once bewildered and bewildering, seeking and never finding, a wave driven by the prevailing winds to break vainly against the cliffs, her destiny made her the very incarnation of German Romanticism.

But what was German Romanticism, so multiple, so complex, and by its very nature so hard to define?

It was something hatched from individual passions, knowing no law but the realization of the self and of one's own destiny. Turned in on itself, German Romanticism perceived little but the rustling of its own pinions. Impatient of restriction by narrow traditional forms, it forced the gates of a new world of aesthetics. And out of that liberty, that anarchy even, it was to create a style.

A strange and fascinating flowering where the tares and the garden plants flourished together! It could only happen on land that had lain long fallow. And so Germany at the end of the eighteenth century, with all its insecurity, became its natural domain. Absolute princely power weighed heavily on the small German states. An apathetic middle class, the 'Bürgertum', with its ingrown inferiority complex, gave no proof of constructive powers, and the individual was hardly conscious of his responsibility towards the common weal. What a stamping ground for those who thought more of emotion than of reason and prized fancy higher than knowledge!

The signal was given by a new generation. The sleeping pricked up their ears. They heard the new ideals proclaimed, dogma condemned, tradition and religious axioms questioned. They saw new forces making way, like liberated atoms, they discovered poets and philosophers turning their backs on a narrow-minded bourgeoisie and scornfully spurning it.

But anarchic though it might be, the Romantic movement in Germany lost no time in seeking out a homeland and an ancestry: it adopted the Middle Ages. In the pre-Renaissance period it saw as it were the childhood of the human race, from which winged genius could take off for lands undiscovered. Nor did it stop at inspiration, but borrowed the forms to be found in the poetry of medieval monks and knights. This was a dangerous form of *pastiche*, leading in the end to the bad taste of pseudo-Gothic, exemplified in English mock-romanesque stained glass and the German style of interior furnishing known as *alt-deutsch*.

But it also looked for guidance to French philosophers of the Century of Light. We may ask, however, whether the German youth of the early 1800s really knew what 'the reign of reason' meant. It is unlikely. They simply recognized in it those elements which were revolutionary and abstract.

The first symptom of advanced tendencies appeared at Berlin, then the resort of writers of all countries, and a meeting place for countless eccentrics, many crackbrains. The drawing-rooms of Berlin were an uplifting spectacle and a source of inspiration. Here passionate discussion revealed to the young Schleiermacher that a social ideal has to be warmed by human feeling, and the future society of his dreams was to be born of the friendships formed there.

Here too Schleiermacher proclaimed his feminist creed, which women took up with enthusiasm. He and his collaborators on the *Athenaeum*—which Friedrich von Schlegel had founded in 1798—are for making a clean sweep of all prejudices and giving women another motive than that of living purely for men. Schleiermacher even foresees a 'virilization' of woman, which must lead, in his view, to a greater liberty, and *a superior human species*.

The friendship between Schleiermacher and Schlegel was formed in the Berlin *salons* of Rahel Levin and Henriette Herz. It was in 1799 that Schlegel published his *Lucinde*, a fragmentary, irregular novel without chronological plan or sequence, to the astonishment of all who had seen in him only the scholar and the archaeologist. Here all laws are rejected: literary rules which are replaced by improvization, ethical laws, where traditional *mores* are replaced by freedom of morals. *Lucinde* proclaims the new ethic of German romanticism.

In our days, the most intimate description of the sensual life is a literary commonplace; nay more, one may say that it is a prime factor in the modern novel. But at that time such an experiment might dismay the reader by its indiscretion and lack of modesty. Everyone knew that *Lucinde* was a transcription of his own love-life; it was no error to recognize in the heroine of the novel the features of the daughter of the famous Jewish philosopher Moses Mendelssohn, Dorothea, who in 1798 had left her husband for Schlegel. After five years of life together—this was the period when the Romantics were proclaiming the concept of free love—they were married, and both, one Protestant, the other Jewish, were fascinated by the mystical attraction of the Catholic Church and were converted.

Schlegel's union with Dorothea had provoked a landslide of spiteful animosity, as his *Lucinde* had done. Schleiermacher, who held similar ethical views to Schlegel's, published an apology for *Lucinde*. Naturally the Romantics received it joyfully. Schlegel henceforth became the idol of the Berlin *salons*, as Lessing had been hitherto.

How is the fact that Jewish women presided over all the most celebrated of these Romantic gatherings to be explained? It is because the liberating ideas of the Century of Light had aroused the keenest response in women, and above all in Jewish women. How attractive this double enfranchisement was for them! They were freed from the ghetto, to which they had no spiritual ties: it is true that young girls in Orthodox households were brought up to respect festivals and ceremony, but the study of Jewish law and theology was a male privilege, and so it was with a light heart that they stripped off the tradition of their ancestors. On the other hand, they were liberated from that passive female life, which was lived in a backwater, out of the main stream of politics and culture. Now everything lay open to them: prejudices collapsed, the walls of the ghetto crumbled, they had access to the world of life and love, of fraternity with the dwellers in the country which henceforward was to be really theirs.

This then was the beginning of Jewish emancipation. The law passed by the French legislative assembly in 1791, granting citizenship to Jews, was also applicable to the German provinces occupied by the armies of the Revolution. But their moral emancipation was too swift for their social advancement to keep pace with it. They had not only been oppressed, they had been despised for too long; no decree can disperse in a day such deep-rooted prejudice.

Before emancipation, the number of Jews in the towns was limited. They were excluded from almost all the professions; all skilled handicrafts were forbidden them; they were allowed to indulge only in petty trading, the management of money and a few liberal professions. Even then every privilege was the fruit of struggle and contriving. Besides, they were crushed by taxation, levies which had still filled the royal exchequer at the time of Frederick the Great. All resistance would have been a vain tilting at windmills. The Jews had but one recourse; to take refuge in a world of their own. Thus isolated from their environment, the isolation was completed by the linguistic factor, and the use of Yiddish, an archaic dialect of German written in Hebrew characters.

Moses Mendelssohn appeared as a light in the midst of darkness. He shed his rays on Jew and Gentile alike: on the Jews, whom he separated spiritually from the ghetto and among whom he spread the language and culture of the Germans—the more remarkable since he himself had only learned to read and write German as a youth—and on the Gentiles, whom he introduced to the values of Jewish thought. However, his was not a polemical nature like that of his friend Lessing who, in *Nathan der Weise*, had publicly preached the equality of religions.

But the time was not yet ripe for fighting. And citizenship did not of itself resolve the tragic problem, did not give the Jew access to society. There was only one way into that—by baptism. By means of a baptismal certificate—what Heinrich Heine called 'the ticket of admission to European civilization—the Jew could take his part in the political and cultural life of Germany.

If so many Jews abandoned the faith of their fathers in order to break out of the ghetto, who shall blame them?

Many of the intellectual *élite* of German Jewry, who naturally had a greater hankering than the rest for the riches of German and European civilization, took this way out (which was also a way in). Paradoxically, though opened for them by laws which were meant to satisfy their ambition for total liberty, it proved a *via dolorosa*. For, by guaranteeing complete freedom to the Jew, it demanded at the same time that he should renounce all particularities of religion and custom. The revolutionary law of 1791 expressly states: a nation within a nation shall not be tolerated. Formulated thus, how could the long-hoped-for freedom fail to create its tension?

The absence of tradition among Jewish women made for a clear field for all romantic and liberal ideals. While the spheres of the higher nobility and the petty princely courts—with the brilliant exception of Saxe-Weimar—were in general mentally arthritic and devoid of all intellectual curiosity, middle-class circles were obtuse and burdened with prejudice. On the other hand, the atmosphere prevailing in Jewish *salons* was unknown in the rest of Germany. All here was novelty; the human warmth, the expression that knew no restraint, the interest in the individual destiny, one's own as well as that of one's friends. With the passionate curiosity of the neophyte, young Jewish women kept a close eye on events outside the confines of their universe, and made contact with the intellectual mainstream of their time.

These *salons* were also frequented by aristocrats engrossed by culture and free thought. What a difference from their own stiff social circle! Here they mingled with poets, artists, actors, even with musicians, whom they met on equal terms, and who were not there– as Haydn still said in his time—'to amuse the great'. These *salons* also welcomed sympathetically, in the years before the wars or liberation, a number of French guests. And nowhere more than here did the genius of Goethe arouse the veneration of devoted enthusiasts.

The author of *A Journey to Berlin through the Royal States of Prussia* wrote in 1799: 'At Berlin, Jewish women play a great part.' The poles of attraction for romantic currents were the *salons* of Rahel Levin and Henriette Herz—the latter the wife of a Jewish physician. Both were converted, though much later than others, to Christianity.

Let their spokeswoman be Henriette Herz, whose establishment was the rival of Rahel's 'attic', and who in her memoirs described intelligently and not without critical sense the atmosphere prevalent in these Jewish drawing-rooms: 'There is a complete lack of links with tradition, with a culture transmitted from one generation to another, and adapting itself to the progress of the times. But in consequence, we have here a society stripped of all prejudice. The women at the head of it have thrown all the conventions overboard and are indulging in an exuberant freedom of spirit. There is no doubt that this spirit was full of originality, of vigour, stimulating and, underneath its astonishing vivacity, endowed with great depth. Rahel Levin more than any other was its fine flower. She was six years younger than me and most of my friends, but the warmth of her thought and feeling, together with her misfortunes, had matured her early. I knew her from childhood, and therefore I know how she fulfilled the hopes which those around her reposed in her.'

THE ATTIC IN THE JÄGERSTRASSE

It would be wrong to try to define Rahel Levin by cartesian analysis: so it would be to judge her, that 'disorganized genius' as Gentz called her; or, as a recent biographer has done, to enumerate her weaknesses. We should approach her warily, listen to her with understanding, and intercept the waves of her spirit at the point where they touch other beings.

Rahel had no gift for action, she never wrote a book, she never painted a picture. But her intuition was all the sharper for that, her flair, her attunement to the rhythms of her age. Better than any biographer could hope to do, she has drawn her own character: 'I have neither learning nor talent. On the other hand I am possessed of a critical sense which is clear-sighted and personal. I am helped by the strength of my honesty. By the harmony of my faculties, by the indissoluble union of my soul and my intellect, which I watch over with integrity. I am helped also by the boldness of my judgments and my bearing, if I find them right. This is my sole attraction, even the one which arouses love. . . .'

If we are to get down to the meaning of these meditations as well as that of so many other thoughts committed to paper by

Rahel, we shall arrive at it much more easily by intuition than by analysis. For her thought is often hermetic, her terminology inadequate, her grammar wrong. Nor does the beautiful sonority of her voice, which charmed her friends, reach our ears. But yet in her conversation she must sometimes have expressed herself with clarity, otherwise Goethe would not have written: 'Strong in all her sentiments, and yet delicate in her manner of expression.'

But at the bottom Rahel is never in search of a style. For her as for all hypersensitive creatures, the traditional modes of language prove inadequate. In her autodialogues she invents a brand-new dialectic which is sometimes indecipherable. She says that she wants to perceive the inaudible and inexpressible thoughts of others, but she also wishes to avoid a stylization that impoverishes literature. Here lies her true strength: detaching from the depths of the soul its most precious treasures, to do honour, as she says, to that which she loves.

Her style in letters has often been criticized, and very severely at that, by her detractors. Brentano in his sarcastic way described it as 'unfathomably fashioned, crackling like a rusk'; he said as much to her, without circumlocution and without tact; 'What you lack,' he wrote her, 'is a sense of melody; which is why the cadence of your phrases falls together in such a strange manner, and often, even when you are trying to express the beautiful music of your soul, sounds like drumbeats, or the rhythmic strokes of axes in the wood, or the hammering of a woodpecker.'

However, it was not solely from the Romantic vocabulary that Rahel drew her supply of richly decorative expressions: we seem to find in it traces of Yiddish, that fruity and colourful idiom, as it was spoken in the paternal household. When she was a young girl she still wrote letters in Yiddish, Hebrew characters and all.

'The tortures I endured could not have been worse, up to the time I was eighteen,' she wrote. Indeed her girlhood was an unhappy one. Her father, Markus Levin, was a businessman. His money had served to emancipate him, but he could not impart to her the clear certainties of Judaism; still less her mother, arrested in barren traditionalism. It was in the painful atmosphere created by religious orthodoxy and the unfulfilled aspirations to social equality that Rahel had to pass the years of her adolescence. And when she says: 'My youth and my whole life have been outraged and ruined,' she is alluding to her father's despotic character.

No doubt the sufferings of Rahel's youth are closely allied to the troubled fortunes of the Jews in those first years of emancipation. But to explain the force of her will, her ecstatic leanings, her intelligence, as purely typical Jewish phenomena, as all her biographers have done, is too much. It is a very different matter when she shows human pity, and fights passionately in the cause of social justice—no doubt in all this we see the reflex effect of thousands of years of suffering.

Well, what was this celebrated Levin *salon*, known outside the frontiers of Germany? She managed to collect around her some of the celebrities of her day; Friedrich von Schlegel, Schleiermacher, Friedrich and Ludwig Tieck, Wilhelm von Humboldt, Chamisso, Brentano, Achim von Arnim, Johannes von Müller, Jean Paul (Richter), the Prince de Ligne, and for a short time Heinrich von Kleist.

But can her *salon* really be called such—these meetings on the top floor of her father's house, that attic crammed with guests? They all came without any fuss, all brought friends with them. She had no ambitions to be smart, and she imposed no conditions on them; nor would she let anyone impose them on her. She wanted everyone to express themselves in all freedom, without artifice, and above all not in pedagogic accents—'pedantry is what I detest, it taints the air for ninety miles around', she used to say.

The climate is created by Rahel, and it is the climate of Romanticism. Around her the younger generation of Romantics, passionately committed to social idealism and polemic, found their expression. Personalities unfold, flamingly intoxicated with friendship, with what Goethe called elective affinities (*Wahlverwandschaften*). Every bond, every friendship, becomes a religion, revelatory, ecstatic. Jean Paul observed truly of Rahel's attic: 'Here is the dawn of a new era.'

Much as Rahel admired the cool competence of the *ancien régime*, she preferred improvization and the exclamatory gesture to the well-turned phrase. 'Our feelings are infinitely more subtle than our thoughts,' she was fond of saying. Her parties were often lacking in decorum, if we are to believe her contemporaries. Schlegel calls the attic a menagerie, full of bohemians and eccentrics: while Humboldt found it 'not very distinguished'. She herself complains of the behaviour of her guests.

Let us hear what Brinckmann, Swedish ambassador to Berlin, has to say: 'The wittiest and the most exquisite company resorted to her, but without fuss or ostentation.' And of Rahel herself: 'Her whole conversation was an amusing mixture of paradoxes, which were often so true and so profound that people were still repeating them years afterwards.'

But more important than the panegyrics of her admirers who were carried away by that often uncontrollable romantic admiration, is the knowledge we have of Rahel's relationships with her contemporaries, her extreme receptivity which made her one of the most valuable eyewitnesses of the intellectual and literary movements of her time. Heine was on the right tack when he wrote to her, in his pointed ironic style: 'Your mind has signed a contract with our age.' And she herself said, in her very personal manner: 'When God sends me people, I do not lose an atom of their breath, their pulse, their looks.' And God sent her a great number of persons. Conversing with them all, she identified herself with them. Often in offering her own personality, in unveiling the secrets of her private life, her weaknesses, her vanities, she shows the same frankness which she demands of others. But alas, if she makes a complete surrender of herself, the reciprocal gesture will often be lacking; because every personality is unique, and there is no such thing as an *alter ego*.

But there were two people with whom she felt on a footing of spiritual equality: David Veit and Heinrich Heine. The former, a Jewish scholar, a childhood friend of Rahel's, was like her a stranger in a hostile environment, and tried like her to adapt himself to the social *milieu* he had just attained, at the same time keeping his intellectual integrity. Their correspondence, published in two volumes in 1861, offers an interesting testimony for those who would examine more closely the years of Rahel's youth. And later on Heine, who suffered from the same Jewish malady as Rahel, was to be able to transform it, not into tears as she did, but into poetic creation.

There is no doubt that David Veit and Heine had deeper understanding of Rahel than had her husband, Karl August Varnhagen, who adored her without reservations. Indeed he respected her, but could he understand the flame that was to devour her all her life, making her die a thousand deaths?

Goethe was her god and her idol, whose works accompanied her all her life long: 'I have made his riches my companion, and he has ever been my most faithful, my only friend.' The primacy of religious feeling over dogma, the confidence in revealed truth, link her with Schleiermacher; her unshakeable faith in human progress, with Hegel. But she has no taste for the works of Richter or of Tieck. Of Schiller too she is critical, and even exercises her irony in speaking of his *Jungfrau von Orleans*, 'that good Joan of Arc, so highly esteemed'. To be sure it would be quite wrong to try to study the literary history of that day and place by means of Rahel's journal notes and letters. Her critical sense, both positive and negative, is always marked by a passionate subjectivity.

We said she was not a writer, and yet she was so at least on one occasion. Varnhagen assembled all the notes she had made in reading Goethe's *Wilhelm Meisters Lehrjahre*, and published them under his own name, as Rahel asked him to. Goethe was not slow in offering his thanks. He knew very well who was the real author, even if he did not mention her by name in his essay *Benevolent Interest in my 'Lehrjahre'*. Rahel communicates her joy to her brother: 'Do read the last number of *Kunst und Altertum*. It is like being decorated with Frederick the Great's Order of the Black Eagle. Fully rewarded, I wear it over my heart. For it is made out of all the tears I have shed, and swallowed, of all that I have suffered, loved, lived, both good and ill. My heart has reached its bourne. The supreme aim of my ambition in this world is that Goethe should be respected in his lifetime by his contemporaries, adored, recognized, studied, understood.' And in a letter to Varnhagen: 'You know me well enough: I seek no approval that I do not grant myself, I do not aspire to praise. But my secret wish all my life has been one day to lay at the feet of this admirable man my anonymous love and my unbounded respect.' She adds also: 'I have followed my profoundest instincts in keeping my reserve towards Goethe.'

In fact, Rahel never imposed herself on the great man. It was only after long years, at Frankfurt, that she dared send him an invitation. And Goethe came unannounced, very early one fine morning, 'just at the moment when I was wearing a very ordinary woollen wrap, brushing my teeth with red tooth-powder'. She quickly slipped on a padded black skirt 'so as not to keep him waiting'. He came to meet her, 'at his ease, like a high-born prince'. Goethe only stayed a moment, and she, depressed by her improvised turn-out, had but one idea—to remedy what seemed to her a mistake. Once he had gone, she put on her smartest dress 'a pretty white frock with a fine high collar'.

Brinckmann, a regular guest at the attic, had given Madame de Staël an enthusiastic and highly coloured description of Rahel: 'Has she written anything?' she asked. Brinckmann replied: 'No: and I do not think she ever will. Yet I would that with her genius she could inspire a score of writers.'

In 1804 Brinckmann introduced Madame de Staël to Rahel. The two women eyed each other, exchanging courtesies. Rahel's assessment: 'Certainly she is intelligent, but she has not a heart that knows how to listen.' Madame de Staël no heart for listening? Even Heine, always the sceptic, while critical of the influence of A. W. von Schlegel on certain passages of her *De l'Allemagne* (which appeared but a few years later), was enthusiastic about others in which Madame de Staël 'expresses herself directly with all her luminous heart, with all her pyrotechnic spirit, her rockets of startling intellectual folly'. Later, however, Rahel was to come to know Madame de Staël better, saying 'She has the talent I lack'. Which makes us think of that other remark of Rahel's, in which, comparing herself with creative artists, she said: 'But as for me, I was given *life*.'

Yes, life. But what a life, strewn with ambushes, disappointments, unhappy loves!

SHIPWRECK AND SAFE HARBOUR

How are we to penetrate the thick undergrowth of Romantic love, that world of rending self-intoxication, without moral restraint, a world whose inmates toy perpetually with the idea of suicide; how can we see it through the eyes of our day?

Over and above this, the love-letters of Rahel seem to us the very epitome of that indecipherable ecstatic language—as for example when she writes: 'The sweetest words of love, the words of sweetest love, ought to be born of a goddess of youth, from a suffering heart, and flow towards us.'

On two occasions her love-life came to grief; painful experiences which destroyed her lightness of heart, once so characteristic of her. 'One should travel the world on foot and not on wheels, in company with wise men or gay rogues, and one should always be having new affairs, and lively ones.'

Besides, Rahel's opinions on love and marriage are so freely and so bravely expressed. Europe, according to her, suffers from three blemishes: the slave trade, war, and marriage. This rejection of conventional marriage she shares with Schleiermacher and Schlegel. Anticipating public opinion by well over a century, she recognizes no difference between children born in wedlock and out of it, and even thinks that legitimate children should bear their mothers' surnames.

Free will alone is virtue, Rahel proclaims, thereby emulating the French philosophers. And so she admires the love-life of certain women of her time who have been able to free themselves from all conventions. She envies Dorothea because she has found it possible to live with Schlegel without any other bond than that of love. She feels herself profoundly drawn to that beautiful, if trivial, Pauline Wiesel, mistress of Louis Ferdinand, Prince of Prussia, the hero whom youth adores: 'You live your life,' she writes to Pauline, 'because you are brave and lucky. But I have to invent my life, because I never have any luck and I lack courage.'

Who knows, perhaps Rahel is armed against misfortune, equipped to welcome good luck, but the latter has passed her by? She is not pretty. Not even striking. With irregular features, too large a nose, jutting chin, she has nothing of that carefree air which gives youth its freshness. But her eyes are beautiful, her look kind and intelligent. Her own judgment on herself is almost cruel in its clarity: 'As I am not pretty so too I am lacking in inner charm.'

But was she really lacking in charm, else how could she attract and fascinate everybody? What we may very well believe is that she lacked feminine instincts.

At twenty-five she loved and was loved by young Count Karl von Finckenstein, to whom she represented everything of which he felt deprived: wit, generosity of heart, moral freedom. Rahel and her circle of friends opened new horizons for him.

For a certain time he managed to bury the world from which he came, that narrow world, bounded by prejudices of caste, which was smothering him without his being aware of it. Gratefully he wrote to Rahel: 'You have freed my soul from the painful feeling of being a cypher. You have brought out the best in me; you have been able to see whatever nobility is in me.'

The engagement dragged on and on. Years passed. Finally, family considerations won the day. In the family seat, the castle of Madlitz, Count von Finckenstein's sisters demonstrated the impossibility of such an alliance: a young middle-class girl without a dowry—and a Jewess! Rahel could have fought back, she could have regained her hesitant suitor. But true to herself she wanted no half-measures, no compromises. She broke off the engagement. But at what a cost! Varnhagen was to write later: 'All her life, she felt that break like a wound.' And Rahel: 'I lived through this terrible thing only because it did not kill me.'

She said herself that she was the greatest virtuoso of misfortune. Two years went by, with an interlude in Paris, before Rahel experienced 'the greatest crime in her life', her passion for don Raphael d'Urquijo, who was an attaché at the Spanish embassy in Berlin.

Rahel plunged head and ears in love with a man who—there is no doubt from the evidence of contemporary witnesses—was not worthy of her. Yet, blinded by passion, she wrote him burning letters: 'I give you the greatest proof of my incorruptible heart. My whole soul throws itself into your arms. Regardless of what you do. This is the genuine love, this is the way that impetuous magic manifests itself.' Later she wrote: 'I lied. The most beautiful lies are those of truly great passion.'

Urquijo with his ferocious jealousies tortures her. Worse still, realizing Rahel's superiority, he tries to humiliate her. When she complains of his lack of respect for her, he answers: 'Finckenstein treated you the same way, so this is no novelty for you.' All the while this affair lasted it was nothing but 'a slow assassination', as she called it.

At this point there enters the life of Rahel Friedrich von Gentz, a diplomatist and well-known writer, a deadly enemy of the French Revolution. His intelligence is fascinating but his duplicity and cynicism repel.

Gentz admires Rahel, perhaps he is even in love with her.

He writes her countless letters brimming with enthusiasm: 'By the living God I swear you constitute the eternal type and archetype of the bountiful tree of life, for all those who have still a spark of sense and spirit.' In another letter written in the same year (1803); 'How often have I told you you are the first being on earth? Who could love, think, write, with your exaltation, like you?'

All this does not prevent him saying, at the same time and in letters to other people, that Jewish women *without exception* are incapable of true love.

Gentz wrote later that she should have 'sent Urquijo to the devil. It was fundamentally—whether on our part or on nature's—an incredible error for us not to have been able to love each other, by which I mean complete and genuine love.' In fact, both had stopped short at a loving friendship. 'Had I insisted on getting what you used to call "the little bit more", we should have lived through an affair such as is rarely seen in this world.' So wrote Gentz when he was already embroiled in the murky currents of the anti-Semitic movement and Metternich's reactionary politics.

The year 1808 was a decisive one for Rahel. She got to know August Varnhagen (only later did he discover from the family archives that he was entitled to the noble appellation of von Ense). He was captivated from the first moment. 'She came into the room, with her slender graceful figure, her deep and lively glance, with her abundant mane of black hair, in a dark-coloured dress which made her look like a shadow. I was surprised to find that she had a melodious voice that seemed to come from the depths of her soul, and the most marvellous manner of expressing herself that I had ever heard.'

Varnhagen then was twenty-four, and Rahel thirteen years his senior. He had not yet come down from the university, where he had read medicine, followed the courses of Schlegel and Fichte, and tried his hand as a writer, without success. What had this young man to offer Rahel? Who was he, that she should offer to trust her whole life to him? 'I feel the void, the real vacuum in me,' he wrote. 'I can create neither thought nor form, nor explain the relationship of things to each other, nor abstract from them their individual and spiritual values; no spring finds its source in me.'

A cruel self-criticism and one which we find surprising, seeing that one day he was to become an excellent writer, corresponding with the most famous men of his day.

But he was to find the true source of his intellectual activities in Rahel, in love with him and soon to become his mistress. Chamisso, who knew Varnhagen well, wrote: 'Rahel with her prodigious intelligence was Varnhagen's prop and stay, his strength, his spirit.'

But he was not just 'the beggar by the wayside' as he liked to picture himself. From a letter which Rahel wrote to him from Berlin we learn that she too felt herself filled with unexpected happiness:

'How abandoned I feel, how almost ridiculous without you. With you and by your side, I am full of courage. You have taught me to bring my designs to fruition. You are the only person in the world who treats me as I treat others. . . . Be happy if you think anything of me at all and if you find my life and my being exceptional; it is you who have humanized them both.'

After a few months living together they were faced with separation: Varnhagen joined the Austrian army as a volunteer. When they came together again at Teplitz in 1811, their life seems to have been stormy and oppressed by quarrels. Rahel's letters to her most faithful friend, Alexander von Marwitz, prove this. A modern author has seen Varnhagen's jealousy as the cause of these quarrels: Beethoven, then staying at Teplitz, is even said to have been in love with Rahel, and some have identified 'distant beloved', to whom he dedicated a song-cycle in 1816, with Rahel.

However that may be, she returned to Varnhagen, and they were married on 27th September 1814. She adopted Christianity on the very day of the wedding.

Henceforward Varnhagen's life was to be dedicated to Rahel. Who shall reproach this *cavaliere servente*, as a recent strictly moralizing historian has done, for having, in the course of publishing his wife's letters, suppressed certain of them which he wished to keep from the eyes of indiscreet readers? We have still enough of Rahel's immense riches for any biographer to find them inexhaustible.

THE REACTIONARY PHASE OF ROMANTICISM

Let us go back a few years in time. 'Our generation was shipwrecked in the year '06', Rahel lamented. Her circle of friends melted away with the entry of the French into Berlin in 1806. Two years later, the fortunes of the house of Levin were at a low ebb, and Rahel had to move house and seek more modest quarters.

Germany being threatened, reaction was not slow in making itself felt. It is true that Napoleon was welcomed in Berlin as the torch-bearer of civilization. 'It is the victory of mind over matter,' said the triumphant Hegel. Nevertheless a handful of intellectuals saw deeper than that: Napoleon with his growing appetite for domination stifled those liberties of which he had proclaimed himself the harbinger.

That handful of elect spirits began a resistance, especially in Prussia; they found themselves in open opposition to the King and the princes, lickspittles of the usurper. In the midst of this official collaboration, a sentiment hitherto unknown was hatched out: patriotism. In the great hall of the Berlin Academy Fichte declaimed his *Reden an die deutsche Nation* to a crowded audience. This philosopher, famous for his pan-European sentiments, changed overnight into a flaming patriot whose words aroused the conscience of one and all.

Rahel did not miss one of his lectures, and her letters at this time (1808–9) bear witness to her enthusiasm for Fichte's patriotism. She approved without reserve his condemnation of all national arrogance, but also his appeals to dignity and to independence. The state socialism which he proclaimed echoes Rahel's own aspirations towards social justice. The religious idealism of Fichte, eschewing all dogmatism and proclaiming faith in God as the sole basis of ethical belief, allowed Rahel to understand her own moral ideals better and to express her moral concepts more clearly.

But what was the use of Fichte's theses, so powerfully based on reason, while all the time Romanticism, pushed to its logical absurdity, was veering more and more towards the anti-rational? The Romantics were lost in their own arrogance; they proclaimed their own nation sole standard-bearer of absolute truth, they invented the myth of national superiority. They rushed headlong into the abyss to their own ruin, as Nietzsche said, 'into the stupid weakness which is the absolute antithesis of civilization—nationalism'. Or as the Austrian Grillparzer said, even more explicitly:

'Der Weg der neueren Bildung geht
Von Humanität
Durch Nationalität
Zur Bestialität.'

The influence of that degradation weighed as heavily on society as on literature. Writers and poets became charlatans and mountebanks, patriots became forgers of patriotism. It was not enough to offer resistance to foreign domination, not enough to keep alive the flame of true patriotism, the spirit of revolt. To add fuel to that flame, national particularism must be pandered to, and the pernicious ideal of *Blut und Boden*—'blood and soil'—must be suggested to the German people. And with it, hatred must be preached. Of these two, anti-Semitism is born.

Rahel was revolted and profoundly wounded by the prevailing narrowness and intolerance. She wrote: 'I am not a Christian of the newest stamp, nor a fanatical patriot.' The circle around her shrank. More and more alone, she compared herself to Iphigenia among the barbarians.

This nationalism in the making had as its inevitable concomitant what is now called racialism. The Germano-Christian Society founded by Achim von Arnim in 1811 would admit no Jews, not even baptised Jews, for its statutes expressly laid down that only those who were 'born Christian' (whatever that means) were to be admitted. More significant is what it did *not* mean, for its exclusiveness in this direction was its chief *raison d'être.*

Achim von Arnim had often expressed his respect for Rahel in days gone by. But now all was changed. Varnhagen wrote to Rahel: 'Arnim has remembered that you are Jewish, and he has drawn the expected conclusion.' Not only he but also Clemens Brentano and his sister Brettina (the wife of von Arnim) 'remembered'.

Clemens Brentano was a gifted poet and short-story writer who was swept away like so many others by the wave of anti-Semitism. Rahel, knowing Varnhagen's chivalrous impulses, implored him not to avenge her on Brentano, as 'I would rather wound my own heart than that of another. But Brentano's hateful remarks finally exasperated Varnhagen, who in 1813 wrote to Rahel: I boxed Brentano's ears for him. . . . He wept, recognizing his own infamy.'

The war of liberation in 1813 gave the patriotic flame a new direction. Politics, art, literature, philosophy, all had a common aim—resistance. When the call to battle came the whole nation was ready.

Rahel too found herself on the side of those who were fighting for liberty. She left Berlin and took refuge at Prague where she worked as a nurse in the military hospitals. But she cared for the French wounded as well as for her compatriots. 'A wounded enemy is no longer an enemy.' There is no trace in any of her letters or in any note of her journals of animosity towards the French or any remark even aimed at Napoleon, whose genius she admired to the end.

From 1819 onwards Rahel and her husband were back in Berlin, but what a lot of friends they had lost! Prince Louis Ferdinand and Alexander von Marwitz had both been killed in action. David Veit, friend of her childhood, had died during the Russian attack, in the course of his duty as a doctor in a French hospital.

Alas, the liberation of Germany set no minds free. Now came the great disillusion. The smaller princely states sank back into mediocrity. The students who had fought for liberty reaped only ingratitude. And the fact that many young Jewish men had fought bravely, many having been killed in action, did nothing to arrest the progress of anti-Semitism.

The few decades following this make a sad chapter in the history of Germany. Reaction succeeded the fire of enthusiasm. It took the form of bureaucracy, despotism, the repression of all liberal impulses. Above all it ruled in Berlin, once the cradle of progressive ideas. There above all an atmosphere of spying and tale-bearing permeated everything. Police persecution was the order of the day. The heavy hand of censorship was laid on masterpieces of literature: neither Goethe's *Egmont* nor Schiller's *Wilhelm Tell* nor Kleist's *Prinz von Homburg* could be staged.

The literary *salons* of Berlin vanished, to be replaced by noisy gatherings of the new rich, who were content to chatter about aesthetic questions. One island in this morass was Rahel's *salon*, which she called 'my enlarged attic'. Celebrities flocked to it; Alexander von Humboldt, Schleiermacher, Hegel, Leopold von Ranke, and there too were found all those who at that time were the literary glory of Germany: Chamisso, La Motte Fouqué, even Achim von Arnim and Bettina, who had somehow regained the affections of the large-hearted Rahel.

The ties of friendship overcome all, making her forget even the perfidies of Gentz, his moral as well as his political ones. As an adherent to Metternich, he represented the most rigid kind of absolutism. But the July revolution of 1830 in Paris put a stop to his activities, his principles, his vanities. In November 1831 he begs Rahel to sustain him; 'Only give me a few words of consolation! Let some ray of light fall from your generous, luminous soul on the darkness which surrounds me.' And now Rahel sees no more in him than an unfortunate in need of help, who has tried for decades to deceive himself and who, as she says, 'had embraced a lie with all the passion of a searcher after truth'.

Certain biographers of Rahel, putting her on a pinnacle, have called her a prophet. It is true that she herself realized her rare gift for foreseeing events: 'I see them coming as one sees people coming up the street out of the window.' Only a few years after the liberation of Germany she foresaw the disasters which the nationalist movement would bring in its train. In 1817 Varnhagen speaks to her in a letter about Franz Theremin, pastor of a protestant parish in Berlin: 'It seems Theremin is become totally pious and hopes the extermination of the Jews is at hand.' Rahel answers: 'Poor devils like him can readily turn cruel; it has long since been proved that weakness leads to cruelty. In the Century of Light madmen like him were kept silent by ridicule; but now we see that their dementia has not been destroyed.' And in the same letter she says: 'Nations are not purged of disastrous error except by massacres. . . . I foresee in my mind a real catastrophe if these madmen are allowed to continue their work.'

She exclaims: 'O poor Novalis! Poor Schlegel, to be still alive today. Little did you expect to see the crackbrains who were your disciples acting as they do. And you, Goethe, the great, the beloved, read by blind men! And you, Lessing, honest and fervent! All you great and serene souls, none of you could imagine this, or foresee it.'

Rahel did have this presentiment. And in August 1819, a wave of anti-Semitic persecution broke like a storm.

'Luckless Cassandra,' Rahel said of herself, in a letter to her brother. 'I have been saying this again and again for the last three years. The Jews will be persecuted. This hypocritical new love for the Christian religion (may God forgive me), for the Middle Ages, its art, its poetry and its atrocities, has moved the people, in making an appeal to history, to the molestation of the Jews!'

Heine's apocalyptic words are aimed at a more distant future: 'The day will come when Germany will see a sight by comparison with which the French Revolution will seem but an innocent idyll.'

The tempest of Jew-baiting was not all that Rahel foresaw, and prophesied. She was equally clairvoyant about the directions which French policy would take. Four months before the July revolution, the future of France was being keenly discussed in her *salon*: 'Beware!' said Rahel. 'The Bourbons will not be able to hold their own.' She was interrupted by Eduard Gans, the founder of German legal philosophy: 'The Orleans will come to power.' But Rahel demurs: 'No, not even they will remain. The French—how well I know them—have republicanism in their blood, and they will not be content until they have a republic. The more I learn about them, the more I am persuaded that the French above all peoples are born republicans. Every Frenchman is conscious of his worth, and wherever the cult of personality is not exalted they are very close to a republican regime.'

The spring of 1821 brought a new familiar, the young Heinrich Heine. Soon he will be calling Rahel's house his home, and he will write to Varnhagen: 'She knows beforehand everything I can tell her, she knows what I feel, what I think and what I do not think.' Rahel said: 'As he was subtle and strange I understood him often, whereas others had no idea what he meant.' Unfortunately the majority of Rahel's letters to Heine have been lost. But we know his reactions to these letters and the feelings of affinity to which they gave rise in him. In July 1826 he wrote to Varnhagen: 'Reading her letter, it was as if in my sleep I had got out of bed; still in a dream I looked in the mirror and talked to my reflection. . . .'

There is no doubt that Heine occasionally showed her his manuscripts, for Rahel wrote to Gentz: 'He has chosen me as his patron. I lavished praises on him, but did not spare a single fault, when I saw his MSS before going to press.'

But in the course of years the bonds of their friendship were loosened. Heine's irony, his sarcasm, his mockery, in the end were too much for Rahel. Ever in search of eternal values, she stands up for her own ideas, but provokes no argument. When Heine is insulted he counter-attacks immediately. Rahel in such cases withdraws into herself like a wounded animal. 'I am convinced,' she wrote to Gentz in 1831, 'that in our life on this earth we are attacked in the most vulnerable quarters. The important thing is how to escape.' Yes, but what was the way out?

The way out of Judaism? 'We must destroy the Jew in ourselves,' she had written, 'even at the risk of lacerating our lives.' But alas, her life was one long laceration.

Moral and physical suffering burnt her up before her time. In 1826 Grillparzer, the great Austrian playwright, met her: she was then fifty-five. He was dazzled when 'this ageing woman, deformed by sickness, looking like a witch or rather a sorceress, began to speak. My tiredness left me and gave way to a sort of intoxication. She talked and talked until about midnight. Did I go away of my own free will or did they turn me out of the house? I do not remember. In all my life I never heard anyone talk so interestingly, so fascinatingly. . . .'

Rahel's thoughts, Rahel's words, uttered in that beautiful German of hers, a medium of brotherhood, which, as Heine bitterly said 'is still a home, even for those who have been deprived of their native land by stupidity and malice.' Rahel, the quintessence of German Romanticism, will hardly dare to call herself German.

Hatred is a poison that seeps into the hearts of those who feel themselves hated, corroding and depriving them of faith in themselves and others. The deadliest side-effect of anti-Semitism is that the contaminated Jews in their turn become the victims of the most terrible moral calamity: they come to despise themselves.

Rahel too suffered this toxic effect. In 1810 she gave up using her surname and took that of Robert, following her brother's example in this. In 1814, on the day of her conversion which was also her wedding day, she exchanged the personal name Rahel, with its magnificent Biblical overtones, for Frederike, a Hohenzollern family name. In her youth she had written: 'I have been taught everything, told everything, except only this: stay Jewish.'

Nevertheless, baptism notwithstanding, Rahel did not become a Christian. In transubstantiation she recognized a form of divine grace, but she only understood it in a symbolical sense: 'God must be re-born in every human being,' she wrote to La Motte Fouqué: 'My religion is anonymous, and I await a revelation from on high.' She waited for the rest of her life, for that 'last act of intimacy between the creature and Him whom I dare not name'.

On the second of March 1833, five days before her death in the year after that of Goethe, she had a terrible night of heart attacks following which she said something of which Varnhagen made a note immediately afterwards: she said she had fled 'out of Egypt and also out of Palestine', and added: 'My greatest shame of all my life, my greatest pain, my greatest unhappiness, has been my Jewish birth, and now I would not be deprived of it for all the world.'

CHAPTER SEVEN

A PRINCESS OF THE REVOLUTION

There is one solitary feminine figure in the Risorgimento; the Princess Cristina di Belgiojoso. She gathered round her, in her house at Paris, men of mark whom she trained for the struggle that was to liberate and unify Italy. In Italy itself, she threw herself body and soul into the resistance against the Austrian oppressor. But the means she adopted to her ideal end were sometimes clear and direct, sometimes obscure and tortuous. Her volatile and glittering personality must in the end remain an enigma to us.

PRELUDE

Cristina was born in 1808, daughter of the Marchese di Trivulzio, whose heroic ancestor, Marshal Trivulce, commander-in-chief under Louis XII, had earned in his lifetime this epitaph: Here rests one who never rested. Like him, Cristina was to live a life of burning heroism and never know rest.

She was only four years old on the death of her father. Her mother married again, to the Marchese Visconti d'Aragona, who was a liberal. As she grew up she witnessed the comings and goings of conspirators in her father's house. They belonged to the Carbonari, a secret society pursuing a political idea based on the primacy of moral liberty. Once it had been in revolt against the French invader, now it pursued a silent clandestine struggle against the Austrian oppressor in Lombardy. But it is a curious fact that it was the French invaders themselves who had brought with them the warm inspiration of the French Revolution, they who had awakened the national consciousness of Italy. Now on the other hand the country was disintegrating under the Austrian terror.

The occupying forces impeded all social and cultural effort. The economy was paralysed, the fruits of Italian labour were drained off to Austria, Austrian products were dumped on the Italian market. Both the working class and the bourgeoisie, in their desire for a quiet life, accepted this order of things with indifference.

However, the spirit of rebellion was brewing in intellectual and aristocratic circles. The Palazzo Visconti d'Aragona at Milan became the rendezvous of the heads of the Risorgimento: Silvio Pellico, who later was to describe, in *My Prisons*, the hell that was Austrian goals, Giovanni Berchet, bard of the partisan struggle, Alessandro Manzoni, the great novelist, Count Luigi Porro, and above all Count Federico Confalonieri, the incarnation of mystic faith in the future, but also of uncertainty and irresolution which damped the ardour of the insurgents.

Confalonieri, more of a cultural reformer than a political leader, was ill suited to the labours attendant on a clandestine struggle. When the great unrest broke out in Piedmont and Lombardy in 1821, Porro and other conspirators managed to escape, but Confalonieri hesitated. His friends urged flight on him, but too late. He was arrested, tried, and in 1824 condemned to life imprisonment, a sentence commuted twelve years later to exile.

Cristina di Belgiojoso was later to expose, in her history of the Lombard uprising, the hesitations of Confalonieri and the weaknesses of the Liberal party. Her clear-headedness, her efforts to lay bear the historical facts without compromise, her criticisms of the dedicated heroes, finally clouded her friendship with certain fanatical partisans. It is only today that the accuracy of her judgment appears in its full light.

How much was known, in other European countries, about these events, or of the slow forces of destruction at work on those imprisoned in the dungeons of Spielberg fortress? Nobody knew that these Italian patriots had to sleep on the bare ground, had to do convict labour, shackled with heavy irons that gangrened their limbs, so that many of them had to submit to amputations.

So young Cristina grew up in an atmosphere of legal prosecutions, of an absolutist régime, of denunications, of clerical reaction, amid the decadence of a people once lively and insubordinate. Bound to the destiny of her country, fortunately endowed with beauty, with intelligence, adored by the young aristocracy of Milan, Cristina at sixteen chose a husband who, like her, had inscribed the name of liberty on his standard. In 1824 she married Prince Emilio di Belgiojoso, who was then twenty-two.

His portraits in youth bear witness to his charm: regular features, fair curly hair, a tender expression, classically chiselled soft lips. But this is in fact the face of a rake without moral scruples.

Was this austere young girl willing to save a damned soul? Would she be able to hold the affections of her handsome prince to whom she was united by political ideals? They passed the first few months of their marriage at Mercato, in a castle towering majestically above the Lake of Como. It was a month of conflict, of the silent opposition of diametric contraries—on the one hand a frivolous materialist, on the other an exalted puritan.

On their return to Milan the Prince took up his old life, and resumed a pre-marital love affair. For four long years Cristina kept up the pretence of a united household; until one night the Prince found himself followed. 'Who told you to shadow me?' he asked the man. The reply was, 'The princess'. Separation ensued by common consent.

It is said that Cristina went about in mourning for her dead conjugal happiness. This is but one early manifestation of her need for theatrical effects, yet perhaps this experience had been the unhappiest of her life. Was it merely bad taste, that public parade of her pain as a woman betrayed?

The question must remain open as must many others that bear on the ambivalent nature of her life.

In the winter of 1829 Cristina was living at Florence, under the seemingly tolerant Tuscan regime, which welcomed political refugees as guests. Despite the network of spies, Cristina had not yet aroused suspicion. She was seen about, at parties, at receptions, at dances. Everywhere she shone by her especial beauty, her body like that of a classical statue, her broad forehead and great black eyes, her highly individual style of dress. 'Hardly yet twenty years old,' writes a contemporary, 'but she seemed to be living a second life.'

Indeed she was living a second life. After the failure of her marriage, she threw herself into another existence, the struggle for the freedom of Italy. Only a few months went by, and then, while she was living in Rome, she was pointed out as the head of the conspiracy. Here she formed her friendship with Prince Louis Napoleon. No matter that he was already working out the means by which he would seize power. Like Cristina he belonged to the Carbonari, his heart beat for her and for the liberty of Italy.

Spies dogged her every step: Torresani, who reported regularly to the Milanese police, Brighenti, who picked up everything she said, Gaetano Barbieri, who signed his secret reports under the name 'Pietro Dolce'. Henceforward the name of Princess Belgiojoso will appear in countless diplomatic papers, in the correspondence between Metternich and his legations, in the archives of the Imperial Chancellory at Vienna, in the Milanese archives of Count Hartig, governor of Lombardy.

Far from withdrawing from this dangerous situation, Cristina welcomes danger and seeks it out. She has all that goes to make up the heroic nature; burning dynamism, disdain of easy living, a spirit of self-sacrifice, magnanimity.

The Austrian government considers whether to arrest her. It seems hopeless to continue her activities on Italian soil. But in the Ticino, where the cantonal elections have brought the liberals to power, Cristina can approach the many *fuorusciti*, the exiles from Italy. But even here she cannot appear at meetings or social occasions, not a word can pass her lips, without all her doings being reported by the *sbirri*.

'Princess Belgiojoso is a madcap,' reported Barbieri from Lugano in 1830. 'She would do better to stay at home and not parade about abroad.'

Meanwhile in July of the same year, revolution broke out in Paris. With the Bourbons overthrown, Louis Philippe is proclaimed king. Cristina decides to leave for Paris.

Throwing off the spies, she goes to the house she owns at Genoa. But the *carabinieri* throw a cordon round it and all the exits are watched. Cristina manages to outwit their plans and escapes by the back stairs. She reaches Nice, and, in the end, by deceit and bribery, succeeds in crossing the frontier. Then in January 1831 she was at last in Marseilles, triumphantly welcomed by the exiles.

They all adored the young woman who was devoted to their ideals and who re-kindled the flame of the Risorgimento.

Cristina wrote to a friend, the Milanese portrait painter Ernesta Bisi: 'To be surrounded by all these grave and solemn men almost makes me laugh. But you know my desire to see Italy great is no laughing matter. That is why I have accepted this troubled, this so unfeminine life.'

On 12th February Cristina in company with other exiles was in the house of an Italian patriot by the name of Fogliardi, when the news was brought to her of the uprisings at Modena and Bologna. Immense joy broke out. Everyone embraced, everyone shouted aloud: 'The dead of 1821 live again! Long live Charles Albert, our future king!' A man jumped on the table, drawing from his pocket a manuscript by Giovanni Berchet:

> *'Sons of Italy, arise! Up and to arms! Take courage,*
> *For this soil is ours.*
> *Arise, Italy renewed, be free and united!'*

The Princess with feverish hands signed drafts for considerable sums of money and besides this she handed over to the expedition which was setting out for Italy from Lyons the proceeds from the sale of her jewellery.

Meanwhile at Paris all was effervescence. Discussion of the events in Italy was in full swing. La Fayette demanded that the Government should subsidize the rebels. He himself sent five thousand pounds to Lyons, where all was now ready for departure. The minister Guizot supplied all those who were leaving with money for their journey. Hundreds of carriages full of volunteers, both French and Italian, converged on Lyons, accompanied all along the road by enthusiastic shouts. 'Long live the Italian revolution! Go and win your liberty!' At Lyons, eight hundred workmen, at Grenoble the members of the city militia joined the convoy.

The spy Svegliardi reported from Marseilles, 'The rebels have left, amply festooned with cockades and ribbons in green, white and red, made up by the fair hands of the Princess.'

Cristina too set out, accompanied by her secretary Pietro Bolognini, a Doctor of Law. The spies reported that she lived with him *in somma intimita*.

On 24th February at Lyons a banquet was organized in honour of the expedition, which had left the day before. Suddenly Ravina, one of the Italian exiles, burst into the dining hall, distraught, his eyes ablaze. He shouted, 'We have been betrayed by Louis-Philippe's government!'

What had happened?

On the orders of the Minister of the Interior, French troops had barred the way of the Italian Legion and the French volunteers as they approached the frontier, and had disarmed them. In the Chamber, the President, Casimir Périer, had declared: 'French blood belongs only to France.'

THE RISORGIMENTO AT PARIS

The scene is Paris, the year 1831. The Princess is living in the city of revolutionary traditions, a city of enthusiasm for the cause of oppressed peoples. But nowadays Paris is also a city with a philistine society, vain and complacent, well suited to the regime of the citizen-king.

Free of all conventions, free of all social ties, ready too to compromise herself for the good of the cause, Cristina seems to ignore the narrow spirit of the bourgeoisie. For her only the future counts, her own country's future. For that future she canvasses without pause sympathizers, and also adversaries, liberals as well as conservatives and reactionaries. She lends aid and comfort to the exiled Italians. From governing circles she hopes to gain support on the Italian Question. In ardent speeches she declaims: 'No, Italy is not a land of brigands and poisoners, a picturesque back-drop for your novelists. No, it is a country groaning under the jackboot of the Austrian occupation, peopled with active, insubordinate men, worthy of your fraternal aid in the struggle for liberation from the princes in the pay of Austria!'

Soon she is seen everywhere; at the dull receptions given by Queen Amélie, at Apponyi's, the Austrian ambassador's (he sends Vienna unfavourable reports about her), at tea with Madame Récamier, who is now advanced in years, talking platitudes to Chateaubriand. She is seen at La Fayette's, where her beauty attracts attention; in the lobbies of Parliament, where she holds political conversations; at the meetings of Saint-Simonian socialists, to which she feels drawn by her faith in a mystical better future.

In the Parisian drawing-rooms with their narrow horizons,

how could she possibly be understood? Fancy an Italian giving lessons in politics to the French! Fancy a noblewoman who does not dress in the fashion of the day! Gossip is in full swing; she takes drugs to make her eyes appear larger, to enhance her interesting pallor! In fact she complains in her frequent letters about the unhealthy paleness of her complexion. The spies' reports take on more and more fantastic, extravagant tones; in them every friendship, every acquaintanceship that she forms figures as a love affair.

But in the eyes of those who share her views it is precisely her freedom from all convention which justifies her. It is on them that the charm of her personality works and it is they who appreciate the genuineness of her political mission. Among the men who meet in her *salon* she finds understanding, admiration, loyalty: Thiers, then Under-Secretary at the Finance Ministry, Mignet, blond and elegant, historian of the Revolution and collaborator with Thiers on the political journal *Le National*, the blind historian Augustin Thierry, who later choses to live in Cristina's house and to be devoted to her for the rest of his life. And above all La Fayette, Commander of the National Guard, hero of the struggle for liberty in two worlds.

No one is more enthusiastic for the cause of Italian liberty than La Fayette. Behind his good-natured countenance framed by a brown wig is hidden a vast passion for political problems, and to be sure for beautiful women too. Stendhal in his *Souvenirs d'Égotisme* speaks of his 'eyes which light up when within a foot's range of a well-formed bosom'.

And Cristina: 'No one who has not lived in close company with the General can have any idea of the charm of this rare and delicate mind, constantly quipping, allied to the most noble and generous heart. Each one of his visits to the fifth floor is for me an event.'

In fact Cristina does now live on the fifth floor and makes her living by writing articles and drawing portraits. This is greeted in the *salons* with smiles; it is thought she is playing a part, putting on an act. But how could she have lived otherwise? On 17th April 1831, a poster on the walls of Milan reads: 'If Prince Emilio and Princess Cristina di Belgiojoso do not present themselves in Lombardy within three months, they will be declared deceased for civil purposes, and all their goods and funds will be sequestrated.'

In her *Souvenirs* Cristina wrote: 'It was my principle that those who have no money should not spend any: but I was like the princess in the fairy-tale who, turned into a country girl by a witch, could neither milk a cow nor knead dough: my efforts at cooking proved this.'

La Fayette, coming from Parliament to Cristina's apartment, was shown into the kitchen first. Together they studied the recipes, playing like children, laughing and finally eating very little. 'I complained that it was a great drawback to have as kitchen-boy the Hero of Two Worlds.'

The old general is head over heels in love. He writes to her: 'The difference between our ages is such that in your attachment to an old friend you are laying up unhappiness for yourself. . . . And yet I have no regrets about giving myself over to this passionate affection, which will have so much influence on what is left of my life, with all the ardour of a young man, with the obstinacy of an old man, and all the self-confidence of my character.'

La Fayette had been won to the cause of Italy long since. Where others only impeded him, Cristina was able to exhort him and galvanize him. Unfortunately almost all her letters to French political personalities have been lost; but the answers echo and bear witness to her power of suggestion. She had unbounded confidence in this homeland of the rights of man, which had declared: 'He who oppresses one nation declares himself the enemy of all.' Yes, Cristina imagined that the French government would defend the cause of Italy before the whole world, and would not hesitate to do so even by force of arms. . . .

Now there enters a man by the name of Giuseppe Mazzini, a lawyer of Genoa. Expelled from France, he was in hiding at Marseilles. Cristina took up contact with him. Alone among the Italian exiles he pursued a concrete aim. His idealism had drawn him to the Carbonari, but he soon found its tendencies too abstract, its paths too heteroclite. So in 1831 he founded a new society, Young Italy, whose programme he defined: no more petty states, no more Papal states, but one single Italy, ruled by the Italian people and with the motto 'Equality and Fraternity' inscribed on its red-white-green banner. This people was to fight on in its partisan war to the bitter end and final victory. The rulers of the petty states of Italy were all reactionaries in collusion with Austria; royalty equalled tyranny. On the other hand, republicanism connoted liberty.

At this point Mazzini's ideas parted company with those of the Princess. He aspired to a republic, she to a constitutional monarchy. She had a premonition that the time for a republic was not yet ripe, that it could find no place in an overwhelmingly monarchial Europe. She came to this realistic conclusion long before Cavour did. But how tragic was her destiny! Forty years were to elapse before her plans were realized.

But one ideal she did share with Mazzini; the end of their struggle was to be an Italy integrated into a unified Europe; the policy leading to that end would be a social but not socialist policy, national but not nationalist, Christian but not clerical.

Not that Cristina was ignorant of the purity of Mazzini's motives. She approved his moral armament, so closely allied to Saint-Simonianism. But her unreserved loyalties, her frankness led her to criticize him. She thought him too inexperienced to hold the reins of the Risorgimento; she, who was only twenty-three, speaks with almost maternal authority of his lack of maturity.

If only the Italian revolutionaries in France had been under a single homogeneous leadership! But even within the circle of exiles itself there were internecine struggles, reflecting in miniature the tensions and dichotomies of the whole Risorgimento. And how often was this struggle fought out in the house of the Princess! All the cream of the exiles met there, but there were as many opinions as there were individuals: the aged Filippo Buonarotti, disciple of Robespierre and fanatical idealist, calling his antagonist Baron Giuseppe Poerio a 'slave of the monarchy'; Count Terenzo Mamiani, a fervent Catholic; the author Niccolo Tommaseo, who, after his departure, continued for many years to correspond with Cristina; Giovanni La Cecilia, that unshakeable republican.

The Committee for Italian Liberation, set up to direct the struggle, had, without consulting the rank and file, published a manifesto:

> 'Thrones are crumbling, crowns are breaking, and on their ruins arises, from the Alps to the sea, the Republic, one and indivisible.'

Of course the Princess had given financial help to the Committee, so she called it to account for its manifesto. She vigorously protested: 'I demand a disavowal of this republican pronouncement, to be publicly made known in the press.' La Cecilia tried to calm her: 'But, Princess, you know perfectly well how many of the reigning princes consider themselves candidates for the throne of Italy, In opting for a republic, the Committee has meant to exclude them all.'

What Cristina herself excluded was compromise. Her thoughts are clear and sober, but her human relationships impetuous and without diplomatic cleverness. Denounced by the monarchists for her revolutionary ideas, by the bourgeoisie for her socialist tendencies, she was radically repudiated by the republicans. To counter-balance these divergencies and correct her own image distorted by the prejudices of her enemies, she should have needed much more virtuosity and even more finesse. As she herself confessed: 'I take every affair brutally into my own hands. I turn it this way and that, and often break it, as children do with toys, to see what is inside; I analyse every feeling to find out the truth.'

Once more the biographer is faced with a riddle: that of the contradiction between the prudent sobriety of her political ideas, the solid workmanship of her writings, and the theatrical and eccentric setting of her private life.

A typical example is her taste in interior decoration: after the sequestration of her property in 1835, she took up her quarters in the rue d'Anjou, in a house like 'a veritable suite of tombs, which seemed to have been decorated throughout by someone in the undertaking business,' as Théophile Gautier wrote.

The drawing-room was a fit habitation for ghosts: walls and furniture hung with black velvet sewn with silver stars; the dining-room decorated with pompeiian frescoes; the studio crammed with crucifixes, holy water stoups, skulls, daggers, on a lectern a folio of parchment, work of some Father of the Church; the bedroom a melancholy symphony in white and silver, with, in the middle, an enormous four-poster bed called by Marie d'Agoult 'the virgin's catafalque'.

Was this artificial and extravagant décor meant to serve the national mission of Cristina, to endue it with a mystic glamour? The whole gallery of celebrities came to it, admiring, excited, criticizing, joking. What is more, politicians came, such as Thiers, Mignet, Cousin, La Fayette, meeting there all the great names in art and literature and music: Gautier, Balzac, Heine,

Musset, Liszt, Chopin, Meyerbeer, Gérard, Delacroix. Lovers intoxicated by her beauty seemed to ignore the redoubtable lack of taste which she showed. For instance Balzac's sarcasm does not spare her: 'She is as much of a courtesan as *la belle Imperia*, but horribly blue-stocking,' he wrote to Madame Hanska, 'yesterday she left her study to meet me, and she came with spots of ink on her dressing-gown.'

And yet, it was in this setting, garish and artificial as it was, that the Princess was struggling to discover the truth. Here she prepared her book on the past of Lombardy, intended to show the historic basis of the present movement for national liberation. Here too she wrote her *Essay on the Foundation of Catholic Dogma*, a theological work in four volumes of lucid thought, solidly based on profound knowledge, but also on subtle intuition. In one particularly brilliant chapter she shows how nascent Christianity takes on the colour of the genius of different peoples. 'This passage struck me as a masterpiece,' Alexis de Tocqueville wrote to her, 'deep in its thought and admirable in its form. You have such a simple and at the same time so elegant a turn of phrase, such ingenious and yet such natural language, that hardly one of our contemporaries can equal it.'

Cristina's letters seem to us equally inconsistent with the pompous setting of her house; letters to her friends, dialogues with herself, all infinitely more revealing than any biography. She expresses her disillusioned thoughts to Tommaseo: 'To live by oneself, with books, with the sun, with God, but not with one's own kind, who impoverish us in showing us their own inadequacy.'

How can this sound and deeply thoughtful aspect of Cristina's nature be reconciled with the attraction which theatrical effects undoubtedly had for her? More than once she is glimpsed, through the open door of her room, kneeling before the altar of her oratory, which is crammed with ornaments, her waxen face lit up by the rays coming through an orange-paned stained-glass window. She was seen even, one day, in the church of the Madeleine, kneeling beside Mignet, while a priest said the office for them alone: they had quarrelled, and the Princess would not make it up until their reconciliation had been sealed by a mass.

The spectacular shows she put on, like certain political ideas of hers, kept her apart from Mazzini. Mazzini's God was not the

One whom Cristina adored, visible to all, or the One who revealed himself to the people of Italy and the world in the course of solemn masses. No, Mazzini's God had no church, no priests, no ceremonies and no laws.

INTERMEZZO

More and more reports about her were being made to the Chancellory at Vienna, police headquarters at Milan, to the Austrian embassy at Paris. By 1833 Cristina could not post a letter abroad without its being intercepted, opened, and commented on, in some official minute. But among the hundreds of sheets of manuscript in the archives we do not find, either in her hand or in that of her friends, a single item suggestive of a love affair.

Is it, as some of her contemporaries claimed, that she meant to make the men who were enchanted by her beauty the tools of her political policy? Men speak to her of love, and she replies about politics. Arsène Houssaye writes: 'She served up the banquet of love with admirable grace, but herself slipped away just before sitting down to table.'

Heine was fascinated by her beauty, which he prized more highly than her political activity or her compassion for the oppressed. He wrote to her: 'I care very little for your heart, which is no doubt a fine one, more or less. All women have hearts, some magnificent ones. For example my grandmother. But none of them have a face like yours. . . .' In another letter: 'You are the most complete person I ever met on earth. Before I met you I thought that people like you, endowed with all the bodily and spiritual perfections, only existed in fairy tales.'

This is how Cristina di Belgiojoso appears in Heine's *Florentinische Nächte*: 'Never shall I forget that face! It was one of those that belong rather to the poetical realm of dreams than to tangible reality: its features recalled Leonardo, a noble oval with artless dimples and the pointed chin typical of the Lombard school. Her complexion was smooth in the Roman manner, with the texture of a pearl, aristocratically pale. . . . In short, it was one of those faces that only exist in paintings of the Italian school, presenting one of those great ladies whom Italian artists of the Cinquecento were so fond of including in their masterpieces, and of whom the poets of that age were thinking when sword in hand and eager for action they crossed the Alps. . . . Yes, it was such a face, across which played a smile of sweet malice and noble boldness, the while that beautiful lady demolished the blond and curly-headed Bellini with the point of her cane.'

Vincenzo Bellini, then at the summit of his fame, had met Heine (whose ironic expression annoyed him) at Cristina's. He whispered, 'That man has the evil eye.' For some reason Heine made him the target of his wit. 'You are young, and, it seems, a genius.' (Heine did not then know *Norma.*) 'All geniuses die young.' Bellini fled amid the laughter of the guests. A fortnight later he was dead, at the age of thirty-four.

At Cristina's musical evenings the Prince di Belgiojoso was sometimes to be found, for he also was living in exile, sometimes at Lugano, sometimes in Paris. He liked to show off his magnificent voice, accompanied at the piano by Rossini. But Cristina despised him, she despised his weak nature, his depraved way of life; he was to be seen drunk in boozing dens, surrounded by his cronies in debauch. The spies reported: 'The Prince behaves scandalously, he has fallen very low in the esteem of the exiles.' Cristina writes to her friend Ernesta Bisi that by giving out that they were reconciled she had managed to stop people talking about them.

In December 1834 the Princess gave birth to a little girl, Maria. She was given the name of the Prince. The question of paternity is not raised in any of her biographies. Two years later Cristina wrote to Ernesta Bisi: 'Not only is Maria adorable, she has the further advantage of recalling the features of a being, my dear Ernesta, who was very dear to us.' She was never to be separated from her daughter.

Idolized by some, decried by others, even the descriptions of her physical appearance are at variance. Here too the truth escapes us. Was she attractive as a beautiful woman present in the flesh, fascinating as a vision from the Beyond, terrifying as a ghost? During a concert, as she stopped in the embrasure of the main entrance, dressed in a white frock trimmed with jet, someone whispered: 'How beautiful the Princess is!' 'Yes,' answered another, 'how beautiful she must have been in life!'

Her eyes seemed to grow larger and larger in her increasingly thinning face. 'So large, so huge, that I lost myself in them and shall never find myself again,' sighed de Musset. She was his *grande passion*, Balzac says sarcastically: 'The Princess Belgiojoso has taken Musset from George Sand, Liszt from Madame d'Agoult, Mignet from Madame Aubernon.' Perhaps de Musset's passion for Cristina was more ardent than that which he felt for George Sand. He and the Princess had more than one point of resemblance: both were hypersensitive and excitable, full of contradictions and conflicts, conscientious and fantastic at the same time.

But Cristina met his passion with sensible, maternal advice. De Musset wanted to run away from his troubles, and never again set eyes on the woman who made him sick with love. In vain, she always managed to call him back.

In June 1846 Cristina had rented a villa at Versailles, where Mignet and Madame Jaubert were staying with her. There she received a note from de Musset, saying simply, 'I love you.' She answered, 'Come.' He stayed a week with her, a week of torment and torture. Cristina, who often suffered from nervous spasms and migraine, avoided being alone with him. He accused her of cruelty and senseless prudery. He reproached her with finding pleasure in torturing him. He was to write to her: 'Who knows? With my love and your friendship God could have done something, but He does not wish to. Now, my suffering is about to make its fearful useless effort by itself. . . .'

That same month, a poem by de Musset, *Sur une Morte* (On a Dead Woman), came out in the *Revue des Deux Mondes*,

> . . .
> *Elle aurait aimé, si l'orgueil,*
> *Pareil à la lampe inutile*
> *Qu'on allume près d'un cercueil,*
> *N'eût veillé sur son coeur stérile.*
> *Elle est morte et n'a point vécu;*
> *Elle faisait semblant de vivre,*
> *De ses mains est tombé le livre*
> *Dans lequel elle n'a rien lu.*

ACTION

'Revolution now!' cried the Italian resistance, impatient and impetuous. 'Softly, softly,' answered Cristina, counselling them to wait, to advance slowly, to prepare the ground beforehand for revolution. The time is near, but the hour had not yet struck.

The *Gazzetta Italiana*, which she founded in 1844, was conformist and moderate, totally at variance with the movement of passionate revolt directed by Mazzini, Young Italy, and this difference too constitutes a tragic aspect of the Risorgimento. The Mazzinians cried treason. After only two years the *Gazzetta* ceased publication. But before that a new magazine had been launched by Cristina, *l'Ausonio*. Designed along the lines of the *Revue des Deux Mondes*, it was of a very high cultural standard. Famous writers, all great figures in the resistance, contributed to it: Massimo d'Azeglio, Alessandro Manzoni, Terenzo Mamiani.

But in the eyes of the exiles, even *l'Ausonio* lacked fire. Cristina however went her own way; from the *adagio* she passed to the *appassionato*. The moment has come, she proclaimed in burning articles, when the whole world should learn how the oppressor has destroyed Italy and stripped her of her artistic treasure, smothering every cultural movement, bringing about a total decadence of literature and art. The exiles, impressed by this note, pricked up their ears; the enthusiasm of her friends was multiplied.

Cristina's collaborator in this venture was young Gaetano Stelzi (the spies said he was her lover), a gifted and sensitive man, but in the last stage of tuberculosis: his portraits show him genuinely handsome, with large romantic eyes in a pale face. He travelled throughout Italy, writing articles on current affairs for *l'Ausonio*. Spies followed him step by step, well in touch with his activities.

Now Cristina is thirty-seven. How much longer will her great burning eyes be an infallible weapon in the war she is waging? From the fortress of Ham, where French political prisoners were confined, Prince Louis-Napoleon wrote to her in the summer of 1845: 'It takes courage to stay shut up between four walls for nearly six years. If only there were a pair of eyes like yours here, that would help to warm this icy air.'

The decision was soon taken. Louis Napoleon was a member of the Carbonari, and had fought against the Pope during the bloody uprising in the Romagna; what would he not do for the liberation of Italy? He must be incited to escape.

On 18th September Cristina arrived in the neighbourhood of the prison. Her carriage was bogged down on the muddy road. As far as eye could see stretched marshy pastures, a foul mist steaming from them. A great gloomy hulk of a building, with a tower at each corner, rose up before Cristina: the fortress of Ham.

The drawbridge rose, the portcullis opened. Cristina went into the courtyard. She was at once led to the cell where the great man's nephew, surrounded by books, newspapers, busts of Napoleon, and of Josephine, was dreaming of future power.

'Prison and prisoner alike made a painful impression on me,' Cristina wrote in her *Souvenirs*: 'Louis Napoleon was riddled with rheumatism. He lodged in a little cell with barred windows, the walls dirty and damp, miserably furnished and musty-smelling.'

She attacked at once: 'How can you live here without attempting to escape?'

'That has often been suggested. But I would rather stay here in my own country because escape could only be followed by exile.'

'But *is* a prison one's own country? As for you, Prince, how can you entertain a forced and irrational love for a country which you left when a child, and to which you have only returned in order to enter this dismal dungeon?'

'But then, it is my duty not to desert my companions in captivity.'

'But you yourself are the cause of their captivity! If you escape and flee the country, the others will automatically be set free.'

But Cristina knew the true cause of his hesitation. 'A young laundrymaid had been planted in the prison, charged with amusing and consoling the prisoner. The girl had done her work so well that the Prince by then was the head of a numerous family . . . there was much laughter in high places at this method of discouraging escape. . . .' The 'numerous family' in fact consisted of two sons whom the Prince, when he became Napoleon III, raised to the dignity of Count.

Shortly after this interview Louis Napoleon managed to escape disguised as a mason and fled to England. After the Revolution of 1848, when he was back in Paris, Cristina went to see him. 'If you are elected, what will you do for my country?' she asked. 'Do you remember how you used to breathe fire and slaughter against Louis Philippe, at the time of the popular outbreaks in Italy, in 1831?'

'Can you have any doubt,' cried the future Emperor of the French, 'that your country will be one of my first objectives?'

He added, in an unctuous tone: 'You will be pleased with what I shall do.'

'But once in power,' wrote the Princess, 'he let the Italian affair drop. The former prisoner of Ham, not content with striking the word amnesty from his vocabulary, took to incarcerating political prisoners in the fortress of Belle-Isle.'

1847. Austrian oppression has reached a critical point. In Italy there is a state of ferment. Pamphlets circulate, conspiracies are hatched—here and there attempts are made at assassination. This exasperates the occupying forces, who become more arrogant and provocative. At Milan, the opposition passes the word around: do not smoke, tobacco is an Austrian government monopoly. Immediately General Radetzky issues tobacco in vast quantities. Officers stroll in the streets of Milan, each with two cigars in his mouth. An Austrian major was heard to say aloud in a café at Brescia 'At Vienna, a life cost five florins, at Milan it costs five halfpence.' 'And here it costs nothing,' cried a man, leaping forward with a dagger and stabbing the major dead.

During this time of troubles the Princess travelled incessantly up and down Italy, for the ban on her residence there was temporarily suspended. Everywhere she preached hate and rebellion, the crusade against Austria. She was seen, still accompanied by Gaetano Stelzi, at Rome and at Florence, at meetings of resisters. Now at last the scope of her articles, her manifestoes was recognized, and the good sense of her political programme understood, with its insistence on the fusion of all the parties.

One of her letters in which she spoke openly of revolution was intercepted. But how were they to arrest her? Only in Lombardy would the Austrian authorities have the right to do this, but she did not show herself there. The traffic of letters between Metternich, Radetzky and the spy Torresani grew thicker and faster. Radetzky, in 1848, asked indignantly: had not the Government a remedy in demanding the extradition of the Princess who was inciting to warlike acts?

Insurrection broke out at Milan on 18th March 1848. The insurgents threw up barricades of paving-stones, carriages, furniture. The tocsin sounded and the people were unleashed. The Austrians opened fire on the rioters. Count Hübner, Austrian envoy at the Court of Milan, watched bloody fighting that lasted for five days. He notes in his journal: 'An infernal din: Radetzky's artillery playing bass.'

At that time the Princess Belgiojoso was staying at Naples. Instantly advised of developments, she felt only one desire—to take part in the struggle. She hired a steamboat, and at once thousands of volunteers appeared, begging to be taken to the scene of action. Almost ten thousand young Neapolitans applied, but there was room in the steamer for only two hundred; it was full in the twinkling of an eye.

Of this throng of volunteers, some belonged to the aristocracy of Naples, some were simple workmen. One of them was a young engaged man due to be married the next day. Five Venetian officers turned up, deserters from the Austrian ship anchored in the Bay of Naples. All came without preparation, just as they were, ready to hurl themselves at the enemy. The hearts of Neapolitans soon catch fire, especially when the first rays of the spring sunshine are bathing the city in a golden light, and a beautiful woman appeals to their patriotic feelings.

The day had been warm and sunny. At five in the afternoon Cristina, as she drove on to the quay, could see the sun glinting on the arms of her volunteers. The s.s. *Virgilic* was surrounded by hundreds of rowing boats, while from all sides rose the prayers and supplications of those who wanted to be taken on board. As the steamer cleared the harbour, enthusiastic cries of 'We shall follow you' were raised.

At Genoa, on 31st March, Cristina and her volunteers disembarked, to be frantically welcomed by the population. The part taken by those first two hundred volunteers from the South in the Lombard insurrection ranked as a national event and became a veritable crusade. The newspapers were filled with accounts of the enthusiasm of the crowd, of the endless applause which greeted the Princess when she appeared on the balcony of the *palazzo* which housed the provisional government.

Count Hübner as an Austrian saw the matter in a somewhat different light: 'An immense gaiety reigned at Milan. Was it caused by victory on the field of battle? Not at all. It was due to the Princess di Belgiojoso and her fourscore young Neapolitans.

Our carriages were held up by the approach of the procession, and so I had the opportunity for a close look at the heroine, whose acquaintance I had made previously at Paris. The last ten years had not gone by without leaving their traces on her face. But she was still a handsome woman. She walked solemnly, holding aloft a tricolour flag, at the head of her young men from Naples. From balconies and windows countless handkerchiefs waved, and the air resounded with cheers. In the Piazza San Fedele, in front of the Palazzo Massimo, the procession came to a halt. Casati came out on to the balcony, presented the female warrior, who was in tears, to the crowd, and made an enthusiastic speech.

'The heroes took some five days to fit out and provision, and then they left for the front. Three weeks later this doughty company, reduced to twenty-five miserable ghosts, were to be seen begging in the streets. Surely they had never come within sight of the enemy, but had indulged in such orgies of looting in the countryside that the peasants had done away with a good many of them with their pitchforks. This is the end of that demonstration that was meant to be patriotic. No doubt the Princess will find some other pastime to console her.'

Italian eyewitnesses give a quite different account again: the volunteers are said to have fought like lions, having cut the enemy's communications with the fort of Castelnuovo along the road from Verona to Peschiera, defended the passes of the Alps and prevented the Austrians from getting there. However, Cristina herself admitted that they were lacking in discipline and that there was no co-ordination between their different detachments.

Charles Albert of Savoy had brought fifty thousand Piedmontese and Lombard soldiers to the front. As Cristina wrote, his strategic plans would have done credit to Frederick the Great, if only military science had made some progress since his time. And everywhere the 'fifth column' was at work; local authorities in villages and small towns provisioned the Austrians, and not the Piedmontese army, besides which they provided them with information about troop movements.

Meanwhile the Venetians, having turned the Austrians out of the port, proclaimed a republic, set free the great heroes of the Risorgimento, Tommaseo and Manin, from prison. The young republic too appealed to the Princess for her support—and this is a proof of the confidence which the Italian insurgents had in her willingness and ability to help them. Tommaseo, co-opted as minister, asked her in the name of the provisional government of Venice to get him ships and arms.

Cristina was then staying at her property at Locate near Milan. The situation in the town was getting serious. The provisional government was showing irresolution, there were rumours of discontent in the army, there were differences of opinion between the republicans and the partisans of King Charles Albert, which weakened the will to fight. Besides, the police force was composed of individuals in the pay of Austria.

The Princess was oppressed with cares. She saw with anguish Stelzi, her ever-faithful companion, growing weaker day by day. He died on 16th June, at the age of twenty-seven. Cristina laid him out herself, and asked the local authorities to have the leaden coffin taken at night to the cemetery of Locate, sealed. She wrote to Thierry: 'I did not know I loved him so much.'

In August the Princess was at Milan, while Charles Albert and his army were in full retreat, falling back on their camp in front of the Porta Romana. In the town, a Committee of Defence was in session. Cristina tried to establish contact between the Committee and the royal headquarters, undertaking to transmit all messages exchanged. Would the King defend the town? Already the sound of Austrian artillery could be heard; up went the barricades again. There was a second Austrian entry into Milan. Charles Albert capitulated, evacuating Lombardy and signing an armistice with Radetzky. He preferred to abandon the town to the enemy rather than ally himself with the republican democrats and defend Milan as its people would have wished. Cristina wrote on 1st September: 'He into whose hands we gave the destiny of Italy has basely betrayed us.'

Prince Felix Schwarzenberg became City Governor of Milan. He ordered severe punishment for all rebels, the sequestration of their property and heavy fines. At the head of the list, mulcted in the sum of eight thousand lire, was the Princess Belgiojoso; but she had already escaped and fled to Paris.

In September of that tragic year of 1848 gendarmes searched her villa at Locate. They opened every cupboard and press, every drawer and trunk. In one of the cupboards they found the embalmed corpse of Gaetano Stelzi, dressed and undamaged. They went to the cemetery and opened the coffin, which was found to contain only a log of wood.

Here is another riddle in the life of Cristina: had she wished, in her love for him, to keep beside her the body of her dear one? Or was this the morbid obsession of a neurotic mind?

At Paris Cristina took up the threads of contact with the exiles, but now, after the capitulation of Milan, after her sad experience of the king in whom she had reposed such hopes, she understood Mazzini much better. On his part, Mazzini renewed his confidence in her. From Lugano, where he was the idol of the exiles, he wrote: 'We do all we can for the support of Garibaldi and his partisans, the only people who still do honour to the national flag.' He asked her to establish contact between the French government and the Italian resistance.

But Cristina was no longer a young woman who by her beauty could fascinate men and lead them to take part in her struggles. Still she had some resources left, and powerful ones; her passion, her almost superhuman energy, her brilliant style and persuasive words. She made appeals to French deputies, she wrote articles exposing the Austrian cruelties in Lombardy, she wrote books about the evolution of her country.

Nevertheless the history of Italy remained confused in European eyes for, as always in the past, the country seemed lacking in unity. As for events in Lombardy, Austrian agents had spread innumerable distorted and falsified accounts. No one wanted to listen to the exiles who were the only people who could tell the truth of the matter.

Meanwhile the rebellion was still in full swing at Rome. The Italian flag still floated over the Doges' Palace at Venice, and enthusiasm still ran high at Piedmont. But these were hard times for the Risorgimento. Charles Albert's neutrality had cooled the democratic fire and the fervour of the patriots; while Pius IX, the hope of the liberals, had just discovered that the Austrians were Catholics, hence creatures of God, and consequently under the protection of His earthly vicar.

Cristina's conversations with her French friends were painful and disappointing. It was now nearly twenty years since she first came to France, during which time she had daily fought for the liberty of her country, writing interminably, launching newspapers, making ardent speeches. 'What am I doing still here in France, where they speak of us as savages?' she wrote in March 1849 to Tommaseo.

Just like Louis Philippe, who had turned away from Liberalism, Cristina's friends abandoned their republican ideals. The slogan of the Piedmontese, *Italia farà da sè*, finally gave France a pretext for non-intervention. And in Paris, where the Republic had triumphed at the cost of bloody sacrifices, Napoleon the Prince Imperial was elected President. La Fayette was dead, Cristina's friend Thiers had joined the reactionary camp. What had they won, she and her companions in exile, in the country of the Rights of Man? There they were with empty hands.

Now suddenly France struck them an even harder blow. Revolt had broken out in Rome, the Pope had fled, Garibaldi and his partisans had entered the City, Mazzini forming one of the Triumvirate—but the French were for restoring the power of the Vatican, French troops landed at Ostia, and laid siege to Rome.

The Princess hastened to Rome to nurse the wounded. She improvised a military hospital in the papal palace on the Quirinal. She gave orders in her calm clear voice; she instituted a strict discipline, herself overseeing the nursing care. The Italian patriots, heroes of the resistance, were groaning and dying before her eyes. There they lay, suffering and perishing of wounds inflicted by French bullets, perhaps fired by the same French soldiers who ten years later would be their allies against the Austrian army; how absurd!

On 2nd June 1849, after heavy street fighting, the French broke into Rome. Mazzini fled, the cardinals triumphed. Cristina remained. She who had cared not only for the partisans but also wounded Frenchmen and priests, was surely entitled to protection. This proved to be an error. A priest who had been stabbed by a workman in mistake for a traitor, had been nursed in hospital by her. After convalescence he was employed on the staff of Cardinal Antonelli. On 31st July a letter was slipped into Cristina's hand. It said: 'Flee with all speed, there are reports about you on the Cardinal's desk, minuted in his own hand in the margin *anti-religious sentiments*.'

Cristina fled that very night. But where was she to go? Return to France was impossible. She wrote to Thierry: 'There is a sea of blood between France and me, and I shall not cross it except in case of dire necessity.'

EXILE AND OBLIVION

Cristina was now little past forty, but seemed much older; her face was ravaged by the struggle, her body emaciated, her dress uncared for. 'It passes me what interest we should take in life,' she wrote, 'when no eye looks on us with love.'

With her daughter Maria and her governess, she took ship at Civitavecchia for Asia Minor. She was in flight not only from the enemy but from her friends and from herself. The Milanese authorities had again seized her fortune, this time on the personal orders of the Emperor Franz Josef.

With what was left of her capital she bought a farm in Anatolia. It was a failure. She tried to make a living writing articles for the press, and even by doing embroidery which she sold through a bazaar at Constantinople.

The articles and books which came from her pen at this time are worth reading, not only her observations on political and social conditions in Turkey but also her views on the Turkish woman; the whole is redolent of Cristina's need to be always bringing a fresh breeze to people and affairs, in a reforming spirit.

In her exile, a last misfortune, and the greatest of all as it proved, afflicted her. She was attacked by a servant whom she had dismissed, and gravely wounded by two stabs with a knife. The worst of these took her in the nape of the neck.

Terribly aged, with her head bowed on her chest, the Princess returned to Europe, having been absent two years.

Meanwhile Turin had become the headquarters of the Risorgimento, and all the patriots rallied there. At last all the most incongruous elements had been assembled in a united programme of resistance by a producer of genius: Cavour, minister under Victor Emmanuel, the successor of Charles Albert.

'All of a sudden the eyes of Italians were opened,' wrote Cristina, 'and they realized that rivalries and contradictory tendencies only brought weakness with them. One and all they recognized that the only form of state that would be able to conciliate the opposed interests was monarchy.'

But who now remembered that thirty years earlier the Princess had worked out a realistic scheme of policy, clear-cut and precise, identical with that of Cavour? Who now remembered her passionate efforts in aid of a fusion of all parties, which presented a striking analogy with Cavour's tactics?

At Turin she had long interviews with Cavour. The partisans returning from France had tried to blacken Napoleon III in his eyes, to brand him as a traitor. From the Princess Cavour heard another side of the story. Unquestionably the Emperor would support an Italian monarchy, if necessary by force of arms: he had promised her as much.

In July 1858 the decisive meeting took place between Cavour and Napoleon at Plombières, and as its consequence France declared war on Austria some months later. In June of the following year, at Magenta and Solferino, the French and Italians were victorious. The greater part of Italy, except for some minor cessions of territory to the French, was united under the sovereignty of Victor Emmanuel. Once more we perceive the clarity of the Princess's vision as she writes: 'The cession of Nice and Savoy had aroused bitterness among many of us: but little by little they will come to understand that the sacrifice was indispensable to our independence.'

In 1868 she published a book on the present state of Italy and her future, an astoundingly modern work, with clearly progressive ideas. She demanded schools for the vast body of illiterates, claimed equal pay for men and women, and the setting up of consumer co-operatives attached to factories, for cultural centres where workers could listen to concerts and organize their own choral clubs. This was a bold gesture by a woman of genius, but it, too, came many decades too early. Her enemies raised the cry of socialist Utopia.

The year 1871 brought the accomplishment of her dream. Italy became a united kingdom, *from the Alps to the Sea.*

She was only sixty-three, but already the tragedy of final decline lay over her. The friends who came to visit her in her palace at Milan or her villa at Locate, were terrified by her appearance: a Fairy Carabosse, draped in strange raiment, wearing diamonds on her all but bald head, toothless, dozing in her armchair, only shaken out of her torpor to take an occasional pull at her Turkish hubble-bubble.

The Risorgimento had conquered, but she who had held high its torch was abandoned, swept aside by her erstwhile companions in the struggle.

In June 1871 she was buried at Locate, as a 'Benefactress of the poor'.

Misunderstood, betrayed, forgotten.

CHAPTER EIGHT

JULIETTE ADAM: OR, THE EUROPEAN TRAGEDY

Thiers said to Talleyrand: Prince you are always talking to me about women. I would rather talk politics.
Talleyrand: But women *are* politics.

Early in the year 1858 a young woman submitted a manuscript to a Paris publisher. It was called *Anti-Proudhonian Ideas on Love, Woman, and Marriage.*

The publisher leafed through it rapidly. Its maturity of style, its dash and its penetration fascinated him. 'Accepted,' he said.

The young woman who was the author bore the name of Juliette La Messine, her maiden name being Lambert. She had early managed to get hold of the three-volume work by Proudhon: *On Justice in the Revolution and the Church.* This book had been banned immediately on publication. The very evening it came out, not a copy could be found in the bookshops. Proudhon the author had fled from justice and escaped to Belgium.

What else could he do? In the midst of the reactionary slough that was the Second Empire, Proudhon had been bold enough to establish the theory of a revolutionary political economy, and to range himself against the privileges of capital and corruption. But his ideas, advanced as they were, were still confined by traditional concepts; the only form of government he recognized was monarchy. More anarchist than socialist, he remained blind to woman's longing for emancipation. The chapters on love and marriage made a great impression on Juliette La Messine. She rebelled: how dare Proudhon proscribe her idols, Marie d'Agoult and George Sand? Giving only the reason that they had preferred individual liberty to the slavery of marriage? So Juliette sat down to write, and write. . . . She examined the Proudhonian theories of moral, intellectual and physical inferiority on the part of women, and opposed to them, by a sort of mathematical equation, sober antitheses stripped of all romantic phraseology.

Indeed, Juliette's spirit was that of the age. An age when the flames of romance had been doused, the adventure of the Great Love was no longer the order of the day. One must be temperate, reasonable, with both feet on the ground.

Juliette had had to school herself to this sense of reality, for the climate of her childhood did not predispose to it. Her father was a dreamer, a socialist of the old school, a man of 'forty-eight; her mother a prosaic person, living down-to-earth; while her grandfather was a good trencherman, often merry with drink but never actually drunk. Her grandmother was a romantic lady who had absconded on the eve of her wedding-day in her night-gown: her fiancé had found her and brought her to the altar just as he had discovered her. In the house of Juliette's father there were so many tensions and quarrels that her mother left her dreaming husband and took the child to live with her grand-mother.

As for all middle-class families of the period, especially in the provinces, the springboard to social advancement was a good matrimonial match. The Monsieur La Messine who asked for the hand of seventeen-year-old Juliette in marriage was only a lawyer from Soissons, at that time, but his career was to bring him to Paris. His fiery temperament—his family origin went back to Messina in Sicily—and his brilliant conversation impressed the family. Juliette's father, foreseeing the Napoleonic *coup d'état*, put all his hopes in his future son-in-law, who was anti-monarchical and had 'the blood of the *carbonari* in his veins'.

Juliette resigned herself to the marriage. But life with her husband was a hell. He was vile and cynical. 'I believe in everything, he in nothing.' Her grandmother came to live with them but he turned her out of doors. Soon Juliette discovered that he was cheating her, squandering her dowry and using it for dubious speculations. After five years of marriage Juliette left him and went to live with her parents and her little girl Alice.

In her *Souvenirs de Jeunesse* Juliette describes her arguments with her father. He told her: 'All I want is the people, and nothing but the people, for a sap runs in their veins which is dried up in us, a vitality that we have lost.' She said: 'As for me,

I want a republic, a new Athens ruled by an aristocracy drawn from the masses and embodying all that is best in them.'

In her novel *Païenne*—one of many that she was to write later—this new Athens serves as the setting for her own personality. But the neo-hellenism of Juliette Lamber, her pseudonym, bears as little resemblance to hellenism as her future private religion did to Christianity. She always narrowed down the vast horizons of the world of the spirit to the limits of her personal vision.

Païenne is a significant reflection of her own narcissism; beyond all doubt she portrays herself there in the person of Melissandre, noble citizeness of an aristocratic republic. But Melissandre does not move solely in the sphere of an ethereal hellenism. She is a woman of flesh and blood, married to Monsieur de Noves, a rake who, like Monsieur La Messine, has squandered her fortune.

No doubt, given such a husband, her love for the painter Tiburce can hardly be classed as infidelity. In the end this noble elegy issues in earthly happiness: Melissandre sends a message to her lover: 'I learn of the death of M. de Noves, killed in a duel. Is Apollo god? Shall I be your wife?'

Was Melissandre/Juliette to be the wife of her beloved? For we may be sure that this Tiburce is no creation of fancy.

Truth is often more dramatic than fiction. In her *Souvenirs de Jeunesse* Juliette shows the same facts in a more earthly and indeed a more cruel light. La Messine, in Algeria, had been accused of fraudulent speculations. A letter, delivered late at night, apprised Juliette of the death of her husband. She woke her daughter, saying: 'Your father is dead.' Alice ran into her grandparents' bedroom, crying: 'My father is dead! My father is dead!' Overjoyed, they all embraced one another. Juliette telegraphed a certain Monsieur Edmond Adam: 'I am a widow.'

A year later, in 1867, they were married. Edmond Adam, a former Councillor of State but a convinced Republican, had resigned after the *coup d'état*. He was honest, faithful to his principles, judicious, a cultivated person to his fingertips.

In Paris, Juliette was no longer unknown. Her book *Idées antiproudhoniennes* had gained her an introduction to the two women she admired most, Marie d'Agoult and George Sand. The latter, now growing older, saw in her the representative of the younger generation. Juliette Adam was beautiful, enthusiastic, but not at all romantic, taking much more interest in political programmes than in matters of love, seemingly the prototype of new femininity. George Sand was well aware of the difference between her own generation and this one, which had no more illusion than Juliette had. 'When we lived only in ourselves, we had lived through the deepest sorrows and reached heights of the soul unknown today.'

Juliette had never been plagued by the quest for the unattainable summits. The interest she had had in her youth for humanitarian liberalism was destroyed by her autocentric cult and was to end in that acute form of patriotism known as nationalism.

CASSANDRA

At the dawn of her political activity, Juliette did not yet try to stir up hatred. Her role of Cassandra was as yet constructive. Gaining the confidence of politicians, she showed a clever strategy in putting them on their guard against an enemy who had not yet declared himself. She was intelligent and her brilliant conversation forced one to listen, so that it was easy to take sides with her.

There is no doubt that she was one of the few people who were able to smell in the wind the rise of pan-Germanism and its dire consequences to come. As early as 1865 she wrote this prophecy: 'Bismarck is trying to isolate us, to estrange Italy from us, and use his policy to destroy the power of Austria.' In the same year she wrote to Mérimée; 'Bismarck wants to expand Germany in order to make Prussia even more powerful.'

Thiers, a Deputy in the Chamber and hostile to Napoleon III's foreign policy, had also said in debate that it was essential to put obstacles in the path of Prussian policy and so prevent the alliance of Italy with Prussia. But Juliette, as always, was well informed. 'Too late!' she cried, on reading Thiers's speech. 'Too late! The Italo-Prussian alliance is already a foregone conclusion.'

She was right. The warning had arrived too late. Ah, if only France were not so buffeted by contradictory currents! Juliette was only too well aware of this; the republicans with their narrow patriotism, the reactionaries trafficking with the socialists, together made up a foggy political atmosphere in which France went off course.

The discussions in the Adam *salon*, in the Rue de Rivoli, reflect this clearly. Juliette, already thinking of what people would say of her after she was dead, transcribed them all sedulously in her diary. It is not surprising to find that she represents herself as leading the discussion. To her life's end she was infatuated with herself—and she lived to be a hundred. But it must be said that her memory was infallible and her notes, despite their egotistic colouring, do not actually falsify history.

Her customary guests were Nefftzer, Girardin, Spuller. Nefftzer was the founder and manager of *Le Temps*, one of the most conspicuous enemies of Caesarism. *Le Temps* was a moderate organ, and by that very fact was one of the leading supporters of republican thought. Émile de Girardin, a famous journalist but somewhat under cloud on account of his speculations in the field of publicity, was faithful to the Empire, but for all that won the sympathy of Juliette by his hatred of the Prussians. At the house in the Rue de Rivoli, he took the chair with his lectures against Bismarck: 'That modern Attila is capable of unloosing the barbarian hordes.' Spuller, a lawyer and a democratic republican, was alive to the Prussian danger, and agreed. But Juliette, even more clear-headed, thought she knew whence the danger threatened: 'First of all we must fight in France itself against the tendency to sympathize with the Prussians. The agents of Bismarck are everywhere among us.'

In June 1866 the Austro-Prussian war broke out. Venetia was abandoned to Italy. Paris was illuminated in celebration. Liberals rejoiced in the weakening of Austria by Protestant Prussia, the clericals sympathized with Rome. Plainly, contradiction had not yet reached its logical extreme. And Juliette herself, once an anti-clerical, having battled passionately in the cause of secular education, began to veer a little to leeward; she sees in the Prussian victory an affront to Catholic France and prophesies that once Catholic Austria is beaten, it will be the turn of France; figuring, one might say, as a Catholic anti-clerical, not a Protestant anti-clerical.

In the German territories a slow transformation was in train. The victory at Sadowa did much to reconcile Bismarck with the Left. As the Liberal stream ran ever thinner, the nationalist channel swelled. But France herself seems to ignore these all too perceptible portents. There is a naïve faith in the anti-Prussian forces which certainly still exist in Germany, but about whose strength people like Juliette Adam have no illusion.

Marie d'Agoult, a great European, foresees that Juliette's sympathies are about to take a nationalist turn. Juliette complains of Marie's growing coolness towards her, and at the same time she exults:'In my *salon* the hotheads of the nationalist faction increase more than in hers.'

1867. The International Exhibition. Resorted to by all nations, this was the last pyrotechnic of the dying Empire, full of the joy of life and feverish agitation. 'What blind folly!' Juliette exclaimed. The march-past of French troops aroused admiration, especially the handsome colour of the uniforms. But the cause of the greatest sensation was the exhibit by Krupps of Prussian industry: a heavy gun.

From her balcony Juliette watched the Emperor's guests pass in procession: The Tsar Alexander II, the King of Prussia, Bismarck, Moltke, the King of Sweden, the Emperor of Austria, the Sultan of Turkey.

She was indignant to see a performance of *The Grand Duchess of Geroldstein* while the Exhibition was in progress. She sent a note to Mérimée: 'Our Prussian guests have had royal amusement, for in this comic opera Offenbach makes fun of the French Army.' Mérimée replied: 'Not at all. Bismarck laughed at the antics of the German courts, since he knows better than anyone else how ridiculous they are. He was not laughing at France, but at Germany.' And so they quarrelled. Mérimée ceased to take off his hat to her.

Soon Gambetta, who was to become a great statesman, and to direct the fortunes of France, entered the life of Juliette. From this time forth she foresaw the importance of this man, who was already being talked about in connection with a great political trial. The Adams would have liked to ask him to the house, but Gambetta had been described to them as a boor, lacking in manners. However, his influence as leader of the republicans increased from day to day, and Juliette and her husband sent him an invitation to dinner.

Gambetta came; with his large powerful frame, his head on its massive neck, a one-eyed Cyclops, whose single orb glittered with passionate ardour. He had thought, in Juliette's own words, to find himself at a gathering of Blue Stockings, and so he came in extreme undress: 'Dressed in something between a greatcoat and a frock-coat, with his waistcoat buttons done up awry, and one of his flannel shirt-tails hanging out.'

That night at the Adams's a select company of smart people were assembled: gentlemen in tails, monocled, buttonholed, the fair Juliette in evening dress, deeply *décolletée*. But her assurance and poise caught Gambetta's eye. She sat this unkempt individual at her right hand. And after dinner Gambetta whispered to her: 'Madame, I shall never forget the lesson you have taught me.'

Soon Gambetta was to become a domestic familiar. Elected to parliament with a huge majority, he demanded social reforms, the right to freedom of assembly, and freedom of the press. His differences with Juliette now began. She taunted him with his liberalism. He retorted: 'You listen too much to Ollivier.' Émile Ollivier, the son-in-law of Marie d'Agoult, stood for an enlightened imperial policy. To be sure, Juliette, with her sound instincts, perceived the fallacies of this conception. Nor was she alone. Mérimée too, despite his loyalty to the Emperor, was painfully aware of the abyss towards which they were heading: 'We partisans of the Empire have been lulled into a false security, we have disarmed France and left her to her fate.'

But how many were really in the know? Only one man, Marshal Niel, like de Gaulle before 1939, really appreciated the state of military unpreparedness in which France found herself. He pressed for more modern arms, more serviceable equipment. But who listened to him? Who even took the trouble to read the German press and note its growing aggressiveness?

Juliette Adam was disconcerted by the short-sightedness of the republican opposition which, pre-occupied with the enemy at home, neglected the menace from without: 'We confuse imperialism and militarism, and to discomfit the monarchists we weaken the fighting strength of the Army.'

In the midst of these sombre meditations, Juliette heard people in the street below singing a song from Offenbach's *Brigands*:

We are the bold gendarmes
Guardians of hearth and home
But by the malignance of fate
We always arrive too late.

'Oh yes,' she sighed, 'we always arrive too late.' The song obsessed her, until she exclaimed: 'I have always loathed

Offenbach for mocking my Greek gods and heroes, and here I am, humming his refrains!'

Opposition to the Emperor was growing. His enemies openly called him a coward and an imposter. What had happened to the popularity of this imperial couple? From her window Juliette had observed that as Napoleon passed by, not a single hand waved in homage.

There was no stemming the revolutionary flood, or holding the seething working class in bounds, or preventing strikes. Pitiless reprisals only redoubled hatred. Repression of the republicans reached its zenith when, defamed, accused of treason, they were made an easy prey for the persecutors.

George Sand's estate at Nohant became Juliette's asylum. Here disquieting news reached her. Prussia had subjected several German states to her overlordship. But still there were people who wished the Prussians well, still there were idealists who believed in peace! Juliette wondered how one could possibly lull oneself into believing that all was well, now that the Prussians were actually publishing maps with new frontiers marked on them! Bismarck had just said that a war with France would be the best means of arriving at the unification of Germany.

Prince Leopold of Hohenzollern, influenced by Bismarck, offered himself as a candidate for the crown of Spain. The Duc de Gramont, Minister for Foreign Affairs, called this a *casus belli* in Parliament. 'With your support,' he assured the Deputies 'we are ready to fulfil our duty without hesitation and without giving way.'

Edmond Adam wrote from Paris to his wife: 'On reading this speech, Bismarck is supposed to have said: here is my war.'

The Prince withdrew his candidature, but Gramont demanded an official declaration of renunciation from the King of Prussia. Juliette was furious: 'This is playing with fire.'

Her fears were confirmed: the King rejected the demand, in the celebrated Ems telegram to Bismarck.

Juliette, staying with George Sand at Nohant, received a letter: 'If Gramont does not give in, it will be too late. The King of Prussia and Bismarck consider that the moment has come to make their war.'

The Ems telegram, made all the more hostile by cuts in it from the hand of Bismarck, was grist to the mills of Napoleon III. The decadent Empire and the reactionary clique saw in it the pretext for war, which they hoped would refurbish the former imperial lustre by victory on the battlefield.

Gambetta tried once more to save peace, but the Ems telegram had made him, too, defiant. His was among the votes granting military credits.

Émile Ollivier, who had been Minister of Justice since 2nd January, uttered the sadly famous words in the Chamber: 'War is a necessity. My colleagues and I accept responsibility for it with a light heart.'

The session of 20th July was an historic one: France declared war on Prussia. Arles-Dufour, a Saint-Simonian and a friend of Juliette, wrote to her at Nohant: 'Our representatives are as lightly ready to cheer for peace as they are ready to cheer for war. But what they are now applauding is nothing less than the mutual butchery of so-called Christian peoples.'

Mérimée to Juliette: 'We have soldiers but no generals.' This was a fact. It soon became apparent that France had gone to war without any preparation. All was lacking: ammunition, artillery, transport. The supreme command had not even enough ordnance maps.

At Nohant letters came to Juliette, speaking of a new wave of enthusiasm in the Army. 'At last,' she exclaimed, 'the word fatherland, so long forgotten, rises to our lips!' George Sand said: 'God grant the Revolution may come without fighting on the barricades. But whatever may be, Prussia and Napoleon III must be destroyed first.'

It was her last day at Nohant: in the streets reservists were singing 'Back to the Army again'. At Paris, patriotic fervour mounted. At the theatre, at the opera, in the night spots, the *Marseillaise* was being sung. More and more the cry *'Vive la République'* was being heard.

In fact the Republic was to come to life: but at what cost!

WAR

It was August, 1870. The Germans were drawing near to Paris. Flaubert wrote to George Sand: 'What is the use of science? This people rich in scientists have committed abominations worthly of the Huns and worse than theirs, for they are coldly systematic, gratuitous, arbitrary, not having the excuse of famine or cold.'

Juliette Adam committed her daughter Alice to the care of her grandparents, in the country. Daily she sent her news, as on the 3rd of September 1870: 'We learned yesterday that forty thousand men capitulated with MacMahon and that Napoleon III is a prisoner—that is what the disaster of Sedan means.' She writes that the Emperor has abandoned to the enemy arms and ammunition but has saved his personal effects, and that the Empress is preparing to flee alone.

Juliette and her husband, moved by the desire to hear the heart of the people beating, mingled with the crowd. It was very thick on the boulevards and round the Opera. Every street-corner was a forum. The Emperor and the Government were insulted. The shout was raised: 'We shall fight to the last man!' Not until midnight did the crowd disperse, and people go home. But not to sleep; windows were lit until dawn.

4th September 1870. Decisive for the fate of France. The Adams were standing in the Place de la Concorde, in a crowd of more than two hundred thousand people. All shouted 'Long live the Republic! Down with the Prussians!' Anger was unleashed against Napoleon III. His crimes, his misdeeds, his failings, all were counted out. The National Guard sided with the people. One will animated the whole mass. 'Here is the true sovereign!' Juliette exclaimed. 'Forgetful of self, devoted to the country, worshipping dignity. This is what Paris offers France, in the Place de la Concorde, this fourth day of September.' Galvanized into action, she made her first public speech here, a speech glowing with patriotism. People thronged round the beautiful young woman burning with the republican cause.

The mob entered the legislative buildings, burst into the debating chamber. Gambetta mounted the tribune: 'Citizens, our country is in danger. Bonaparte and his dynasty have for ever ceased to rule in France.'

The Third Republic was born. A government of national defence was set up, including Gambetta, the soul of resistance.

Edmond Adam was appointed prefect of Police: and he and his wife moved to a flat in the Prefecture.

While the hospitals were admitting hundreds of wounded, the rumour went round that a new defensive line was being established. But the growl of the guns grew nearer and nearer.

Already the Germans had infiltrated into the suburbs. 'The Prussians are at Montrouge,' Juliette groaned. The siege of Paris began on 18th September.

On 26th January 1871 Juliette Adam wrote: 'An armistice has been signed. At eleven o'clock the forts will cease fire—but there is still shooting now. By midnight the guns will be silent. I should like to be dead by then.'

Next day: 'The Prussians have marched into Paris, under the Arc de Triomphe, and they have passed the portals of the Louvre. But the crowd of Paris closed in behind them, swept away all traces of their presence.'

The siege had lasted four months. In March 1871 the people, exasperated by their hardships, rose in revolt. The Federation of the National Guard seized power and the insurrection of the Commune broke out.

'Hate has been redirected,' wrote Flaubert, and indeed its target had been changed: the fear of the 'Reds' was so great that in the Assembly even the Republicans changed their tactics and made overtures to the Bonapartists. And Thiers, who under the Empire had fought for the Republic with fanatical fervour, sent the Army to suppress the revolt of the Commune.

Between George Sand and Juliette understanding was no longer possible. George Sand wrote in 1872 to Edmond Adam that she wished peace for all nations, including the Germans. And yet, she says, there is in France a party that wants to carry on the war at all costs: 'Patriotic it may be for all I know. But it is inhuman.'

'What a bitter disappointment,' sighed Juliette. 'A great gulf has opened between me and my friend whom I loved so well. She has become again the humanitarian she was in '48.'

Peace was signed on 10th May 1871. The Treaty of Frankfurt aroused a wave of nationalism. By it, Germany annexed Alsace-Lorraine and one and a half million Frenchmen. By imposing this treaty which so humiliated France, Bismarck sabotaged true peace.

REVENGE

Vae victis! Of military defeat was born a tragedy even more dire in its consequences. The peace treaty gave rise to an obsessive feeling of inferiority, and provided a forcing ground for the psychosis of revenge.

The republic had been restored but was one only in name. The monarchical idea still kept its prestige, still the reactionary elements of the Second Empire were on the alert and hostile to the republican government.

Opposed to this reaction was a new movement, motivated by patriotic republicanism and not at all warlike, represented by Gambetta. His bitterness over the loss of Alsace-Lorraine was expressed laconically but in words which went to the heart: 'Never speak of it, think of it always.'

Gambetta's patriotism was humanitarian, diametrically opposed to that of Juliette. It is true that she followed republican ideals, but their strength was as nothing compared with the hatred she bore the Germans.

Shortly after the end of the war, the Adams reopened their *salon* in the Rue Poissonnière. Old friends were reunited there, but also new ones were found, such as General de Galliffet, the bloody liquidator of the Commune, hated by the Left, and General Boulanger, a warmonger thirsting for revenge.

Gambetta not unjustly feared a monarchist *coup*, and was preparing resistance to the Government's reactionary measures under MacMahon. But Juliette Adam saw in Gambetta's constructive policy only a weakening of the idea of revenge. As she brought fuel to the flames, Gambetta protested: 'You are set in your obstinacy, blinkered in your views, coming round and round again to the point of Alsace-Lorraine. You are for the immobility which is death, and I am for the action which gives life.'

'I shall march on towards revenge.'

Sometimes Gambetta is ironical: 'Mme Adam's hatreds are pushed to the point of ferocity.' And Juliette: '. . . or else to the point of foresight which is plainly intolerable.'

Edmond Adam died in 1877. There was no lack of suitors for the hand of the pretty widow. She had promised her husband not to marry again for three years after his death. But who are these suitors whom she mentions in her *Souvenirs*? Gambetta? Did he court her? Did he so much as hope? She certainly harboured jealousy of his mistress, Léonie Léon, and waxed indignant about their connection.

At all levels, the conflict between Gambetta and Juliette Adam grew sharper. She was now even unwilling to credit the sincerity of his patriotism. 'A man who has not a hundred per cent French blood in his veins'—he was of Italian origin—'cannot possibly be a patriot.' Sadly she notes in her journal: 'Ah, if only Gambetta had in his veins the atavistic blood of Old France! In that case he would hardly have found justification for approaching Bismarck by way of La Païva's Henckel. But of course his opportunism is really just another *combinazione italiana*.'

This bizarre combination of proper names is to be explained as follows: Graf Henckel von Donnersmarck had before the war married La Païva, one of the most celebrated Italian courtesans under the Second Empire. But La Païva was an intelligent and cultured woman, not at all the spy which the nationalist clique saw in her. On the contrary, her political aim was to bring about a *rapprochement* between France and Germany. And so Gambetta went to the château of Pontchartrain, where the Henckels lived, hoping to find there support for his policy of *rapprochement*. He did not wish these advances to be made public, however.

His secret did not long remain secret. Juliette Adam heard of it at once. New discussions ensued, this time with Juliette at her summer home at Bruyères, where she held forth indignantly: 'You are betraying your destiny. Bismarck will never make you as great as your fidelity to Alsace-Lorraine has made you. The devil is making use of Henckel and La Païva to deliver you into the hands of the Prussian enemy.'

'Who told you about it?'

'Bear in mind that Henckel keeps French servants.'

Juliette noted in her journal: 'If ever Gambetta shakes Bismarck by his bloody hand, I shall refuse him mine.'

On 23rd April 1878 Gambetta sent a note to Léonie Léon, 'My darling, the Monster is coming back to see me.' The Monster was Bismarck. In fact, Gambetta intended to go to Berlin on 29th April, through the good offices of Graf Henckel, but his journey was to be in the strictest secrecy.

Émile Spuller, Deputy for the Seine, had had wind of the project, and rushed to Juliette: 'You must prevent this interview at all costs.'

On the next day, 25th April, Juliette gave a great dinner. Among the guests were: Gambetta, Spuller, Freycinet, Girardin. After dinner Gambetta asked his hostess:

'Would you cut the cards for us?'

Juliette made the following forecast from the fall of the cards: 'You run a great risk of losing your prestige in this devilish encounter, as dangerous as that of Christ when he was tempted on the mountain. The cards warn you to distrust women and their advice. By all means take a lover, my friend, but go to men for your confidences.'

'As a friend you have spoken ill of yourself, but perhaps that is done in order to speak worse of others.'

'It is only the cards speaking. I see a road that you must not take, for you will find mortal peril along it; including moral downfall and murder.'

'It has always been foretold that I should die a violent death, and at the hand of a woman.'

This is a disquieting remark when we remember that the manner of Gambetta's death has not been fully explained to this day.

In a message to Henckel, Gambetta notified him that he wished to cancel the interview. It would be pointless to add that Madame Adam attributed this action to her dissuading influence.

Her *salon* became a hotbed of hatred. From it, all idea of a possible reconciliation was outlawed. Juliette reacted violently against any participation in the Congress of Berlin, where France would be able to play only a secondary part. In fact, this Congress was to set the seal on the *Pax Germanica* in 1878. But it was an uneasy peace which gave birth to new alliances. The influence of Germany grew greater still, Bismarck incarnating the power of the new Reich. As arbiter of European affairs, he held in his hand the leading-strings of the German Empire.

If Madame Adam looked abroad at all, she did so only in search of a possible instrument in her quest for revenge. Hence her sympathy for Russia. She praised the Romanov regime and rejoiced to hear those voices in Russia which denounced Bismarck as traitor to the old Romanov-Hohenzollern friendship. She tried at all costs to pave the way for a Franco-Russian alliance and challenged Gambetta with her project. 'Spoken like a Cossack,' he said. 'Partnership with Russia in a war would only bring defeat after defeat.'

In 1879 the republican party in both houses became so powerful that the reactionary MacMahon had to resign before the expiry of his seven-year term of office. Jules Grévy was elected President of the Republic, and Gambetta President of the Chamber.

Feverish debates in the Cabinet or in the Chamber were echoed in Juliette Adam's house, indeed discussion was even more impassioned there than in the lobbies of the Assembly.

Gambetta was seen no more at her dinners. Now he moved in Radical circles, and, to the chagrin of Juliette, frequented the houses of those hostesses who were known as *Précieuses radicales*. Though he often came to see her privately, such visits gave rise to stormy scenes. When in 1880 Jules Ferry, Minister of Education, put through the anti-clerical Schools Bill, she tried to incite Gambetta to a counter-offensive.

A total and significant change had come over her. 'The sight of Frenchmen abandoning the idea of revenge had estranged me from Jacobinism and from the whole concept of the Great Revolution.' And thus Juliette Adam, one-time violent anti-clerical and non-Christian if not anti-Christian, explained her conversion to militant catholicism. 'The campaign which is being waged against the Catholic faith in France is only too like Bismarck's *Kulturkampf*.

Gambetta died in 1882, at forty-four. Clemenceau took over the leadership of the Radical party. In the same year Paul Déroulède set up the League of Patriots, the aim of which was vengeance. Despite the affinities which bound him to Madame Adam, he wrote in his *Mémoires* that she was lacking in 'the memory of the heart'. In his judgment she had slandered Gambetta, the soul of national defence.

France and Russia drew nearer together. France aspired to alliance with a country which like herself had reason to fear the giddy aggrandizement of Prussian power. The Russians on their side strained every nerve to gain the ear of official circles in France. Juliette formed friendships with Russian diplomats which were to be decisive in these negotiations. Many historians ascribe the Franco-Russian diplomatic agreements of the years 1891–92 to her influence.

At that time, she had created an instrument powerful enough to make her ideas of revenge known beyond the frontiers of her country; this was the magazine that had been running for some years, the *Nouvelle Revue*.

THE NOUVELLE REVUE

Madame Adam's influence on French politics is incontestable. Besides, her smart receptions were a veritable school for poise. A hostess of note, a woman of imposing presence, still beautiful, she guided the conversation into whatever channel she desired.

Obsessed with the desire for posthumous fame, she had bought land on which she intended to have a street built and called after her, and in fact it is still called 'Rue Juliette-Lamber'. In a world of draperies, bronzes, ceramics, Chinese vases, curios, Madame Adam reigned 'more powerful than any minister', as Flaubert said; sure of herself, intelligent, narrow in outlook, intolerant, humourless, autocratic; the epitome of the French middle class of her day.

For a long time now she had been planning an enlargement of her sphere of influence. What more appropriate than a magazine which would open to a wider public her political ideas and literary tastes?

The *Revue des Deux Mondes*, the very antechamber of the Academy, was then the rock on which the intellectual establishment was founded. Long before that, George Sand had pointed out to Juliette how traditional this magazine had become, how closed its mind was to modern ideas. 'Why should not you found a new review?' These words had sunk in; a new review. Yes, why not? And this was the very title for it: *La Nouvelle Revue*.

The venture was viewed by her friends with misgiving, but especially by Gambetta. 'Can a woman,' he wrote, 'have enough authority, knowledge, energy, and practical know-how to run a magazine?' 'Let me tell you,' was Juliette's answer, 'that for the next twenty years I shall publish a magazine, and that I shall enlist a score of new and talented contributors.'

But Girardin, that old trouper of journalism, was not so sceptical: he was to be among the first subscribers and better still he helped to set up the finance committee, and float the company.

Some writers welcomed the scheme with enthusiasm. And when Alphonse Daudet promised his collaboration, Juliette was transported with joy, exclaiming: 'He, the equal of Balzac and Flaubert, the superior of Zola and the Goncourts, is a spirit of light who can make a hundred images come to life.'

Flaubert promises her the novel he is currently writing: *Bouvard et Pécuchet*. Again, Juliette is enchanted. 'Flaubert is our greatest catch. It is he who will set the seal on it.' Flaubert also speaks to her of his young protégé, Guy de Maupassant, and assured her that any magazine can count it as an honour to publish the first fictional instalments of this 'little man who will go far'.

For the features, Madame Adam secured the best specialists; Saint-Saëns on music, G. A. Thierry on history, Flammarion on scientific studies.

The first number came out in 1879. On the title page was an ardent appeal to 'Our readers. The Germans may have taken us by surprise, but they have not finally conquered us, we shall rally round our national flag. The Gallic order of the day "Live to act" has become ours, and our national duty shall be "act to live".'

From the very first number, Juliette's magazine contained literary treasures. Unpublished letters by Mérimée which proved sensational, letters by George Sand on the events of 'forty-eight, writings by Sacher-Masoch, Sully Prudhomme, Leconte de Lisle. The list of recruits grew longer still: Paul Bourget, Pierre Loti, Maupassant, Richepin, J. H. Rosny, Marcelle Tinayre, Camille Mauclair, Paul Margueritte.

Naturally she kept for herself the department of foreign politics; these articles were clear and sober, but always one-sided, always slanted on the theme of revenge. Her hatred for Germany was so violent that Bismarck, through the medium of a diplomat, complained to Jules Grévy, then President of the Republic: 'Can no one silence this she-devil?' Grévy replied: 'There was one man who could do it, her husband; but he is dead.'

Where did she get her information? No one in France knew. But she had her own secret service; a woman of exceptional ability and perfectly in touch with events regularly brought her all the news from Prussia; she crossed the frontier with documents concealed in the folds of her cloak.

When her sight was not darkened by hatred, Madame Adam had sometimes an astonishing clarity of vision, in foreseeing the political future of foreign countries. A single example will suffice; what she had to say about the Czech question in 1894:

'No one can poison the legitimate passions of a people with

impunity; they [the Czechs] are refused all satisfaction, the enemies of their race are allowed to legislate against them. No one can foresee what will become of the resistance which this people will put up in spite of tyrannous oppression.'

Sometimes her prophetic gift led her even further. In many articles in the *Revue* she foretold the German invasion of Belgium.

She travelled indefatigably about the European capitals, as far as Russia, to study political and social conditions in different countries. Her studies appeared in books which were published with a subsidiary company of the magazine, under the name of 'Count Paul Vasili'. Bismarck thought this author was a real person, and was so enraged by his revelations that he demanded his extradition.

What a useful windbreak the good Count Paul proved. Under the shelter of his name Madame Adam was able to present herself in a more favourable light. In her book on Parisian society she makes Count Paul Vasili say: 'Madame Adam was educated the shyest of Republicans. She trains the most unlikely material in the niceties of costume, and all the appurtenances of smartness. One hope inspires her: to see the leaders of her party become heads of government.'

'The leaders of her party'—that meant the advocates of revenge, and so (to no one's astonishment) she must sympathize with Léon Daudet, who together with Charles Maurras, another anti-democrat and anti-liberal, managed and edited the *Action Française*, the organ of total nationalism.

In his *Souvenirs*, Daudet writes of Juliette Adam: 'She planted in my heart a rational hatred of the German Beast that will not be obscured except with my being.... The quiet, dogged, daily struggle against the Teuton was the framework of her existence.'

Daudet was surprised that Bismarck's agents had not put her out of the way. According to him, it was she who warned the Russian government of Bismarck's war plans, and she even went to Russia herself because she thought her letters might be intercepted.

About 1895 she began to bar 'enemies of France' from her *salon*. From then onwards only Nationalists and senior officers of the services were invited to her dinners.

But this state of mind was confined to her clique. This very decade of the 'nineties was the one in which the true countenance of modern France took shape, the generous French image of which the Dreyfus affair and its final outcome are the true reflection. The spirit of humanitarianism came to the fore, the spirit of those who would not tolerate the condemnation of an innocent man 'to save the Army's honour'.

Of course Madame Adam supported the persecution of Drefus militantly.

But her political part had already run its course. Her literary influence was getting weaker and weaker. In 1899 she resigned the management of the *Nouvelle Revue* but, remaining mentally on the alert, she continued to take a passionate interest in political events.

After the first victory of the Marne, in the autumn of 1914, she wrote in a letter dated 26th September: 'I have been waiting for this moment for forty-four years.'

She still remained hostile to Clemenceau, a man of the Left and a *Dreyfusard*, signing all her letters to him 'Juliette Adam, faithful and constant in her enmity'. But when Clemenceau took a firm stand against defeatism, when he began to preach the struggle *à outrance*, she was ready for reconciliation. And in 1919, when she was an old lady of eighty-three, he sent an Army car to fetch her to Versailles so that she could watch the signing of the peace treaty.

Juliette Adam was disappointed. She thought too many concessions had been made to Germany. To the end she remained shut up within her anti-European policy, ruled by an irrational obsession. It was a policy of moral inadequacy, of intolerance, of national pride, a policy that was to push Europe towards a recurring cycle of tragedies.

CHAPTER NINE

GERTRUDE STEIN, A CONTEMPORARY

THE PICTURE

It is the beginning of this century. At an exhibition of modern art, a man is looking at a picture. He rubs his eyes. What can this painting mean? Here are cubes and prisms and quasi-crystalline forms, and in the chaos of strange contours an eye, a nose, a mouth, as if built into a structure of light and shade. And the title is 'Portrait of Mr X'. The man bursts out laughing, goes away. Other visitors stop, grin and pass by, while others, outraged, try to damage the picture.

Gertrude Stein too had stopped in front of a picture of this kind. But she did not laugh, she understood that she was in the presence of a fascinating adventure, a daring initiative that would rock the past thousand years of humanistic tradition on its foundations. Gertrude Stein welcomed this extraordinary transmutation of values with satisfaction.

What had happened? How came it that the object, the human figure, the landscape, escaped the artist's vision, yet came back to him modified, denatured, decayed, or in some instances vanishing to the point of total eclipse? How is the genesis of this art explained?

Gertrude Stein said in 1906: 'In the twentieth century movement will be the dominating element.'

Movement and rhythm can no longer be kept within bounds, and this will be reflected in art. The true artist, gifted with uncommon receptiveness, is able to capture the rhythm of his age in his works as a glass prism captures light rays.

But modern art, despite its explosive aspect, made a less abrupt entry on the scene than is generally supposed. Like every new style, the art of our day has had its prehistory and its logical evolution.

The visual world of the artist has always been that of his time.

But nowadays mechanization has burst in on it. In the second half of the nineteenth century, when human energy had to a large extent been replaced by mechanical power, painting was undergoing a phase of dissolution. Painters no longer mixed colours on their palettes but laid them side by side on the canvas, leaving it to the eye of the viewer to amalgamate them. The object was replaced by the impression which it evoked—Impressionism was born. Impressionism is the first artistic consequence of an acceleration of life outpacing the natural human rhythm. This new speed became the form-shattering element. The artistic movements following on Impressionism (Pointillism, Fauvism, Cubism), leading to a total abandonment of figurative art, are only parallel expressions of the growing velocity of modern life, the giddy speed of the machine, invented by man and finally dispensing with man.

The patchwork art of the pre-1914 decade did not glorify beauty any more. It had surrendered to the modern muse: her name was Abstraction. Form is dead, long live Form! A form newly revealed, which does not present us with the human face, with the flower, or with the landscape, in just the same way as modern music denies us melody.

The shock of speed had become for the artist a traumatic experience. His relation to time and space is distorted, the visible world no longer comes through to him. The phantasmagoria of the great city, the cacophonous din, nuclear force, flight in space, pulsate in his work.

What, at its beginning, was rejected, was acknowledged as true fifty years later. Pictures that were mocked at by so many, whose worth was recognized only by visionaries with the viewpoint of Gertrude Stein, now hang in galleries, admired alike by connoisseurs and laymen, enjoying the sanction of the state, ranking officially as Art. Public money has been spent on them.

Gertrude Stein intuitively foresaw the creative spirit of modern art. This earth, she said, was not the same in the twentieth as in the nineteenth century. Why? Because you can see it from an aircraft. And even if the artist is not flying over it, he has a new perspective.

She herself experienced this new vision: '. . . going over America like that made anyone know why the post-cubist painting was what it was. The wandering line of Masson was there the mixed line of Picasso coming and coming again and following itself into a beginning was there, the simple solution of Braque was there . . . .'

Modern art as Gertrude Stein saw it is what we see today also. It is a barbarous and dangerous art, but fascinating for all that. Is it beautiful? Does it have to be beautiful? It is, like it or not, the mirror of our time.

GERTRUDE STEIN BECOMES GERTRUDE STEIN

Born in 1874 at Allegheny, Pennsylvania, dying in Paris (or 'Paris France', as she would say), Gertrude Stein belonged in her own words to 'a very respectable middle-class family' of German-Jewish origin. The youngest of five children and the darling of her parents, spoiled by her brothers and sisters, she said that 'One should always be the youngest member of the family. It saves you a lot of bother everybody takes care of you.'

She claimed that she had told all about her family in her book *The Making of Americans*. All? Well, no—in that natural history of a variety of *homo sapiens*, nearly a thousand pages in extent, there are no facts, no palpable statements. She herself called it 'a description of how everyone who ever lived eats and drinks and loves and sleeps and talks and walks and wakes and forgets and quarrels and likes and dislikes . . . '. It contains a minute description of her parents, which is not in fact their description, for she saw no point in remembering them: none at all. The whole is written in her characteristic style, sentences without syntax, without punctuation marks, full of staggering contradictions.

But we do have the sources, her autobiographical works written in a comprehensible style, full of facts, events, humour and pert reflections, especially the one she wrote in 1933 and which was translated into French among other languages: *The Autobiography of Alice B. Toklas*. In it she speaks through the lips of her life-long companion, Alice B. Toklas, which allows her to mention Gertrude Stein all the time in the third person, with complete freedom.

But even in her books we discover nothing of her private life or emotions. Not in these books. The figures that move in them are artists, writers, art-lovers; they revolve in the closed universe of Gertrude Stein.

Two people had a decisive influence on her early youth: her brother Leo, two years older than she, and the philosopher William James. With her brother she went to Cambridge, Massachusetts. Leo attended, as he would say, Harvard University: she, Radcliffe College for women. The subjects in which she majored, biology and psychology, shaped the course of her intellectual development; she 'came out of the nineteenth century' and consequently 'had to be interested in evolution and biology'.

The ascendancy that her tutor William James, brother of the famous novelist Henry James, had over her, is incontestable. Later she tried to apply his theories of rhythm as it affects linguistic expression to the literary form of her own writings.

William James had advised her to follow the medical course because it would give her a more solid basis for her study of psychology. So she put herself down for the faculty of medicine at Baltimore, the Johns Hopkins Medical School. But medicine bored her, the abnormal repelled her, and she failed her examinations. She acquired the knowledge to write her story *Melanctha* only by serving as a nurse in a maternity home for coloured women; she called this story the beginning of her revolutionary work.

From 1903 onwards she and her brother lived in Paris. She said that America was her country and Paris was her home, that was how it was and that was how it had to be. And so it was to be. They settled in the Rue de Fleurus in a house with a studio adjoining which was to become her *salon*. For her Paris was the only place for the people who had to create the art and literature of the twentieth century. It was with these people that she was to live, evolving with them and thanks to them. She belonged to the new generation; though a few years older than it, she was yet young enough to understand these artists and mature enough to protect them, rich enough to buy their works.

This was just the period of unrecognized geniuses such as Braque, Juan Gris, Matisse, the period when Picasso was transforming poverty and distress into his 'Blue' compositions. which Vollard, the great dealer, stigmatized as the work of a madman.

Gertrude Stein and her brother often went to see Vollard at his gallery in the Rue Laffitte. Vollard was quite dumbfounded by her outward appearance. To quote from his *Souvenirs*: 'To see her in her coarse corduroy dress, with her leather-laced sandals and her rather smug bearing, one would take her for some housewife whose horizon was limited to her dealings with the greengrocer, the grocer, the dairyman. But as soon as you exchange glances with her, you know all at once that this Miss Stein is something other than middle-class. The sharpness of her look quickly indicates the observer whom nothing escapes. But once she laughs her mocking laugh, as if she were making fun of someone, it is impossible not to be carried away, to abandon oneself to her in all confidence.'

Vollard's appreciation is significant. Gertrude Stein possessed an exceptional gift of observation. But her intuition was far in advance of her intellect. What is one to say of her humour? It glitters and flutters behind the most seemingly serious remarks.

Gertrude Stein records in *The Autobiography of Alice B. Toklas* that: 'Later on Vollard explained to everyone that he had been visited by two crazy Americans and they laughed and he had been much annoyed but gradually he found out that when they laughed most they usually bought something so of course he waited for them to laugh.' Soon they were to buy a great many pictures: Cézanne, Monet, Renoir, Daumier, Gauguin.

In 1906 Gertrude Stein met Picasso. He had settled in Paris in 1904, and lived a life obsessed by work, a moral solitary. His Blue period was drawing to a close. Leo Stein had seen his *Girl with a Basket of Flowers* in the house of Clovis Sagot, an ex-clown who had opened a picture gallery in the Rue Laffitte. But Gertrude did not like the picture; above all she disliked the legs and large feet of the model. Sagot, who was more of a dealer than a connoisseur, suggested cutting the picture in half, so that she could take the top part only. This did not appeal to Gertrude. In the end she let her brother use his own judgment. Leo bought the picture for a hundred and fifty francs. That was the first Picasso to come into the Rue de Fleurus.

Picasso wanted to paint Gertrude's portrait. She was neither feminine nor attractive, but her presence was imposing. So Picasso set to work, and according to Alice Toklas—that is according to Gertrude—'Picasso had never had anybody pose for him since he was sixteen years old, he was then twenty-four and Gertrude Stein had never thought of having her portrait painted, and they do not either of them know how it came about.

Anyway it did and she posed to him for this portrait ninety times and a great deal happened during that time.'

Ninety times Gertrude scaled the heights of Montmartre to the Rue Ravignan and the famous *Bateau Lavoir*. She sat on a rickety chair, and Picasso sat on a kitchen chair. Round them the room was in turmoil, with a fire crackling in the iron stove.

Sometimes Fernande, Picasso's mistress, entertained them by reading La Fontaine's fables. Gertrude Stein's appearance impressed her: '. . . a big stumpy woman, massive, with a fine head and strong noble features, sharply accentuated and regular, with intelligent, clairvoyant eyes, those of a witty person. She had a clear neat mind, her voice and bearing were masculine'.

Thus the portrait such as we know it was born: Gertrude Stein imposing and important, one eye melancholy and the other ironical.

Suddenly Picasso decided to put an end to the sittings. 'I shall not see you again,' he said abruptly, in annoyance. Later, after his return from Spain, he finished the portrait on his own. 'Is it like me?' asked Gertrude. 'One day, you will come to resemble it,' Picasso replied.

Twenty years later Gertrude had her hair cut short like a man's. Picasso looked at her with distaste. He said sternly: 'My portrait . . .' but softening, he added, 'All the same, it is all there.'

In 1938 Gertrude Stein said that he had made her a present of the portrait. She liked it both then and later. To her, it was herself, and the only portrait of her that stayed herself.

After he met the Steins Picasso's life took a happier turn. The first time they came to his studio they bought eight hundred francs' worth of paintings. 'Who would have hoped for this?' cried Fernande.

In fact, Leo Stein, by buying the *Girl with a Basket*, had shown a surer instinct than Gertrude. But it was she and she alone who followed up the artist's evolution; at that time she was alone in her appreciation of Picasso. Leo had nearly killed himself laughing at Picasso's most grandiose picture, *Les Demoiselles d'Avignon*, now the jewel of the Museum of Modern Art, New York; we have Picasso's word for it.

Leo and Gertrude shared their lives for many long years, sharing too their flat, their purchases, and their adventures of discovery. But in the end they wished to live their own lives. The cutting of this fraternal bond had to come, they could not go on looking after each other, but it did not have its effect until they began to express themselves in their own ways, Leo in painting and Gertrude in writing.

Gertrude thought very little of Leo's painting, nor did he think much of her writing. She summed it up by saying that the simple fact was that, of the two, she was the genius; there was no ascertainable reason for it, but it was she and not he. That, she said, was the beginning of the end; they who had always been together began to see less and less of each other, until finally they never met any more. The definite separation took place in 1912. He kept his Matisses, she kept her Picassos, but the break was a vitally important one for Gertrude. From that moment onward she gave herself over passionately to the writing that was her life's work, and queened it alone at No. 27, Rue de Fleurus.

27, RUE DE FLEURUS

No, the *salon* is not a *salon*, and Gertrude is not a lady. Visitors come and go, which means that the ones Gertrude likes can stay and the rest had better go home. Gertrude sits in a hard straight-back chair, all the time swinging her wool-stockinged legs and her sandalled feet; and when she speaks in her deep masculine voice, people listen, no matter what she says. There she sits like the Pythoness of Olympia, imposing on her tripod.

It was thus that Alice Toklas, all the way from San Francisco, found her in 1907. Later Alice moved to the Rue de Fleurus herself and stayed until Gertrude's death. She took over all the housework, corrected her proofs, and embroidered on cushions and chair-covers designs which Picasso drew for her.

She looked after the guests too, saying that geniuses came and talked to Gertrude while their wives talked to her. This tidy-minded American middle-class woman often had cause for astonishment at the tables covered with notebooks, littered with the contents of Gertrude's pockets and those of her brother—pebbles, nails, cigarette-holders, and all. She marvelled too at the huge cupboards and high Renaissance chairs.

It is hard for us to realize that people like Gertrude Stein and Leo Stein, whose advanced ideas were known on the other side of the Atlantic, should have lived in a house so ill-suited to their times. Gertrude explained that if one were intellectually ahead of one's time it was natural enough to stay simple and old-fashioned in one's daily life.

But on the other hand, what walls! Picasso, Matisse, Renoir, Cézanne, Manguin, Vallotton, Toulouse-Lautrec, Gauguin, from floor to ceiling. And, of course, Gertrude's portrait by Picasso, and the *Girl with a Basket of Flowers.*

If there was a knock at the door, Gertrude 'usually opened the door to the knock and the usual formula was, *de la part de qui venez-vous*, who is your introducer. The idea was that anybody could come but for form's sake and in Paris you have to have a formula, everybody was supposed to be able to mention the name of somebody who had told them about it'. On Saturdays she kept open house, and it was always full, with more people than chairs for them to sit on, so that many had to remain standing. Though they invited no one, everyone came. It was always like that and sometimes like that, and when it was like that it was like that.

But the atmosphere is never the same. Gertrude changes the pictures round and freshens up the walls. She tries also to manage a change of guests, to have fresh ones in place of the old, and every new face is a novel experience for her. She said she liked to take a chair and sit in on a human being's life.

Despite her masculine looks, her relations with artists and writers were marked by a feminine approach. To like a work, one must have accepted its creator and absorbed him into one's universe. If she quarrelled with an artist, which happened now and again, she took down his picture; just as she liked, after quarrelling with an author, to publish a sharp criticism of his writings. In her *salon* she did not aspire to any sort of harmonious atmosphere; on the contrary, she revelled in argument and controversy. These were after all not fashionable gatherings, rather meetings of conspirators, plotting against traditional conceptions. And Gertrude Stein was the core of the conspiracy.

Those years before the outbreak of the First World War saw a great flourishing of friendships between writers and artists. Artistic affinities bound together Picasso, Max Jacob, Alfred Jarry, Guillaume Apollinaire, André Salmon. Montmartre was their kingdom. There they worked with a truly religious ardour, in down-at-heel studios, in attics; there they broke out into clowneries by night. Their poverty isolated them from the bourgeoisie and strengthened their feelings of friendship for one another.

Gertrude has a preference for Apollinaire, with his 'head like one of the late roman emperors'. He brought his friend Marie Laurencin to the Rue de Fleurus, and Gertrude found her very attractive. They were a remarkable couple, she with 'the thin square build of the medieval French women in the French primitives'. Her voice was high but marvellously harmonious.

One of the first to discover Matisse, Gertrude had bought his *Woman in a Hat* which, at the autumn *Salon*, had called forth a storm of laughter. Who could be the bold buyer? Matisse wondered. On making inquiries he found out, and acquaintance ripened into friendship.

But little by little Matisse gained a wider public. Gertrude mistrusted his success. She reproached him with having no more fight in him. For all that, their friendship was to last for many long years yet. Until, in fact, *The Autobiography of Alice B. Toklas* came out, with its description of Madame Matisse as 'a very straight dark woman with a long face and a firm large loosely hung mouth like a horse'; that was the finish of their friendly relationship.

Not long before the outbreak of war a change came over Gertrude's Saturdays. The flaming arguments faltered: modern art was consecrated, the exaltation of its birth was damped. Gertrude was conscious of this; the kind of people who came had changed. Then came the war. The circle was dispersed.

Juan Gris, much appreciated by Gertrude, was so depressed that he painted only dark shadowy pictures. Apollinaire, though a foreigner, joined up and wrote patriotic letters from the front. Picasso stayed loyal to the Rue de Fleurus, and brought along Erik Satie, whose sparkling wit enchanted Gertrude. He also brought along an elegant young man called Jean Cocteau. All are in the fever of a new creation for Diaghilev's Russian Ballet: *Parade*, with music by Satie, libretto by Cocteau and décor by Picasso.

For Gertrude war was no catastrophe—neither of the two world wars was. Still, both she and Alice Toklas did some hospital nursing. But cataclysms were beyond the range of her understanding; she imagined that war was movement like a dance or like a bullfight. As for the soldiers, the eye got used to the sight of streets without men in them, only figures in uniform who by that fact were not men any more but soldiers.

When peace came, receptions in the Rue de Fleurus came back with it. Many old friends were no more, others had left Paris. Apollinaire, badly wounded, had died of Spanish flu in 1918; Juan Gris was at the gates of death; Matisse was living at Nice. A temporary estrangement separated Picasso from Gertrude Stein. It was, as she had written, the time when one had no friends.

Yet new faces appeared. Rootless Americans, artists, writers, poets, all converged on Paris. The best years of their lives had been starved of growth during the war. The lost generation, she called them. Hemingway took this formula for the theme of his novel *The Sun Also Rises*, in which these lost people pursue a fictitious happiness in Paris nightclubs and at Spanish bullfights.

What a place of refuge was Paris! So many things were taboo in America; advanced literature, freedom of expression, liquor. . . . In Paris American writers can live and drink as they please, here nothing is forbidden and here they meet the previous generation: Gertrude Stein, Ezra Pound, James Joyce. Gertrude Stein becomes a rallying point for all. A caricature of the 'twenties showing Paris invaded by American authors carries the caption: 'Warning. Alight at Vavin Underground. Next stop Gertrude Stein.'

In 1919 the American Sylvia Beach started a bookshop in Paris under the sign of *Shakespeare and Company*. It too bore the imprint of the lost generation. With her French friend Adrienne Monnier she had done even more than Gertrude Stein to launch young writers, and as Valéry Larbaud says, she had 'carried on the traditions of the Hôtel de Rambouillet'. The culminating point of her efforts on behalf of authors was the original edition, published in 1922, of *Ulysses* by James Joyce, a work considered 'undesirable' by English, American, and Irish authorities. Sylvia Beach and Adrienne Monnier introduced a swarm of young writers to the Rue de Fleurus, among them many Americans of whom Picasso was pleased to remark, 'They are not men, they are not women, they are americans.'

As in pre-war days, Gertrude Stein presided over an odd clique. The atmosphere in this studio-salon had hardly changed, except that the accent of discussion was now more on literature than on art. But still let him beware who neglects to pay due homage to Gertrude, for he will soon be shown the door. She still hated convention and proved it by her badly cut colourless clothes, and by the favour which she showed to couples of the same sex.

How many authors famous in our day rubbed shoulders at the Rue de Fleurus! T. S. Eliot, Sherwood Anderson, Scott Fitzgerald, Ezra Pound, Ernest Hemingway, Louis Bromfield, John Reed, Edith Sitwell, John dos Passos, besides the Frenchmen Jean Cocteau, Valéry Larbaud, Tristan Tzara. Gertrude Stein called Fitzgerald the only one of the young authors who knew how to write phrases naturally as they came, she declared Sherwood a genius, and showed a liking for Hemingway because, as she admitted, he had helped with the publication of one of her first books.

In 1937 Gertrude Stein and Alice Toklas had to leave the Rue de Fleurus because their lease was not renewed. They moved to an apartment in the Rue Christine.

During the Second World War they left Paris and lived a very secluded life, which did not prevent Gertrude Stein from writing a book called *Wars I Have Seen.*

After the Liberation of Paris many American soldiers came to visit them. Thornton Wilder said that many of his buddies came to Paris at the instigation of their buddies, to see the Eiffel Tower and Gertrude Stein.

OUTPOSTS OF LITERATURE

There is no doubt that Gertrude Stein should figure as one of the pioneers in any history of modern literature. American, free of all ties with the older cultures of Europe, she worked her way into a new medium, without hesitation and without scruples. As André Gide said 'it was necessary to be without laws in order to heed the new law'.

In her lifetime her admirers plaited laurels for her, and still today she has her panegyrists who think her one of the greatest writers of our time. They are wrong, because her true importance is in having pioneered the way for an *avant-garde* stylism. And like all pioneers she overstepped the bounds of the possible and the acceptable.

When Gertrude Stein says she has done certain things and

written genuine poetry, novels, essays, what she means by genuine, in our view, is simply the discovery of an archetype, a source from which other writers may draw. Nor did they hesitate to do so. For her, the twentieth century is a natural phenomenon, in which everything is dissociated and detached and destroyed or in the process of destruction, which is why everything is more extraordinary than in a period when things follow in logical sequence.

How is this phenomenon to be explained in literature? Gertrude Stein set out on a new path: she isolated the word, she detached it from its context of thought and feeling, she matched it with other words that she strung together like beads on a string, nor did she vary the pattern by putting punctuation marks between them—above all no question marks. If a sentence begins with the word 'Why', then it must be a question and needs no special punctuation. Only the full stop is allowed because it has a life of its own; it signifies the end of a rhythmic sequence. The paragraph also is admissible as marking the bounds of an image.

And all this before James Joyce, well before Guillaume Apollinaire, who also discarded the aid of punctuation. Unquestionably she was first with this innovation.

Some think that Gertrude Stein chose words according to their colouring. No, her words are achromatic and apoetic. Her intention can be guessed: she wished to create a process of writing allied to that of modern painting and to allow the reader to be carried away by the rhythm of the words. In the course of experiments bordering on the absurd, she invented an alchemy of writing, but the words are nothing but a culture-bouillon in the test-tubes of her laboratory.

In her book *Composition as Explanation* (1926) she explains the necessity for repetition. In order to conjure up the continued present, one must begin again and again, and it is with this object that she wrote the so often quoted sentence 'A rose is a rose is a rose'—an axiomatic declaration of faith which she had engraved as her letterhead.

The sources of her inspiration are fleeting images, human voices, the traffic of a great city. Sitting in her open Ford, notebook and stylo in hand, she listens to the din of the streets and tries to translate it into sentences. Also she tries to perceive every being's personal rhythm and to express it by a verbal rhythm.

This is how she created her many 'portraits', on which she commented: 'I feel with my eyes and it does not make any difference to me what language I hear, I don't hear a language, I hear tones of voice and rhythms, but with my eyes I see the words and sentences and there is for me only one language and that is english.'

Her works have to be read and re-read, and that is what she intended. She wrote to an editor who wanted her to use clearer and more comprehensible language that her work would be of no use if it were understandable at first sight. Excessive as that may seem, she was right. Her ascendancy over other writers made itself felt only retrospectively. She said herself that her sentences got under their skin before they were aware of it.

Certainly she was not hampered by modesty: in *Everybody's Autobiography* she declared that Einstein was the creative spirit of the philosophy of the century, but hers was the creative spirit of its literature.

Gertrude Stein left behind her a mass of writings. Yale University Press was bold to undertake publication of her complete works.

But the accumulation of experience, of experiments, interesting as they are, does not constitute literature. The critics have often been hard on Gertrude Stein. Sometimes her style has been compared with the tom-toms of primitive peoples. Even that story which comes closest to reality, *Melanctha*, was in Katherine Mansfield's view only monotonous Negro music transmuted into prose. And Edith Sitwell, though appreciating her role as pioneer, called her *Geography and Plays* (1922) an uninterrupted irritating chatter.

But despite these criticisms, the hold that her advanced technique had on modern writers was and is considerable. Sherwood Anderson, defending her against attacks, credited her with the role of a pathfinder who had awakened in all writers a new sensibility for the terms of expression. He calls *Tender Buttons* (1914), so much mocked and decried at the time, the most remarkable landmark of its generation. And Bromfield said of *The Making of Americans* that every young author taking his part in contemporary literary movements owed a great debt of gratitude to that book. When *The Geographical History of America* came out, Thornton Wilder wrote to her that her book was inestimable and great, in the same sense that a high mountain was great, and yet as familiar as an everyday walk.

Hemingway acknowledged all that he owed to her. In 1922 when he was Paris correspondent of a Canadian paper, she had discovered his talent. She had asked him what was the use of being a journalist and not a real writer. Two years later Hemingway sent her two short stories, asking, in his covering letter, whether writing was not a difficult calling. Before he met her he had found it easy. Then he wrote badly, no doubt, now he continued to write badly but in a different way.

Gertrude Stein had shown him how to transpose a conversation into images. But it is not easy to define her influence on Hemingway; perhaps it is to be found in his characteristic method of making events roll along as on a strip of film, in a succession of 'takes'; perhaps also in his manner of echoing the same word, the same phrase, that finally comes to have an obsessive effect on the reader.

Later, the relationship between Hemingway and Gertrude Stein deteriorated. She ceased to believe in him. When he had become a famous author, when his books were among the best-sellers, he ceased to struggle, he became, as Gertrude said, a model pupil.

Hemingway took his revenge. In *For Whom the Bell Tolls*, in the course of a conversation between two characters, Robert Jordan and Agustín, he went so far as to blaspheme the famous Steinian rose by comparing it with an onion:

> 'What hast thou against the onion?'
>
> 'The odour. Nothing more. Otherwise it is like the rose.' Robert Jordan grinned at him with his mouth full.
>
> 'Like the rose,' he said. 'Mighty like the rose. A rose is a rose is an onion.'
>
> 'Thy onions are affecting thy brain,' Agustin said. 'Take care.'
>
> 'An onion is an onion is an onion,' Robert Jordan said cheerily and, he thought, a stone is a stein is a rock is a boulder is a pebble.

Did Cocteau take her 'rose is a rose . . .' seriously? We owe to the excellent biography of Gertrude Stein by Elizabeth Sprigge the publication of a previously unprinted poem by Cocteau addressed to her:

> *Gertrude l'admirable*
> *J'ai reçu ce soir votre grand sourire grammatical.*
> *Votre rose qui est dans une rose qui est dans une rose.*

Je ne vous vois pas, mais je vous aime, vous le savez et
J'habite avec vous le pays perdu.
Hélas je comprends seulement à moitié (When half is
May how much is May)!
G. Stein, je suis fier de votre poème et je vous embrasse.
Jean

A melodic cataract of words that issued from Gertrude Stein did find a musician to set them. The American composer Virgil Thompson asked her to write the libretto for an opera. She suggested the subject to him; her favourite saints, Theresa of Avila and Ignatius Loyola. And the action? No, action would be superfluous. Just being a saint was enough. The fact of sanctity was all. The saints are discovered seated, they get up and walk, two other saints join them. The opera is called *Four Saints in Three Acts*, and it was put on for the first time at Hartford, Connecticut, the words being sung by Negroes; it had a great reception from the *avant-garde*.

That same year Gertrude Stein undertook a lecture tour of the United States, in company with Alice Toklas. The audiences were astounded, almost magnetized by the concatenated repetition of words and phrases. They were aware that Gertrude Stein had something to say, that she brought many new and original interpretations to the physiognomy of the word. The tour was a triumph, every session was sold out, Gertrude was fêted and petted, asked to call on Eleanor Roosevelt, surrounded by countless photographers and reporters.

She had the presumption to say that in America everyone was famous but some were more famous than others and she was the most famous of all. But was it presumption? Certainly not in the eyes of those who knew her ascendancy over so many of the writers of the 'twenties. Gertrude Stein was conscious of her role in the outposts of literature; the creative person, according to her, is a contemporary who is aware of that which is contemporary before his contemporaries are aware of it.

INDEX

INDEX